TRANSCENDENCE

FOR BEGINNERS

Clare Carlisle is the author of eight books on philosophy and philosophers, including *Philosopher of the Heart: The Restless Life of Søren Kierkegaard* and *The Marriage Question: George Eliot's Double Life*, which won the 2024 PEN Prize for Biography. Clare grew up in Manchester, studied philosophy at Trinity College, Cambridge, and now lives in Hackney. She is Professor of Philosophy at King's College London.

'Spanning continents and centuries, traversing mountains and seas, this expansive book asks what it means for a philosopher, or a biographer, to work from life. Carlisle's beautiful prose fizzes with illuminating questions, stories and, above all, human connections, as she maps out a powerful and moving "philosophy of the heart."'
— Francesca Wade, author of *Gertrude Stein: An Afterlife*

'This is the book of a lifetime, and a book about lifetimes. What is the relationship between philosophy and biography? How can a line of writing reveal a line of living? Clare Carlisle is a guide and a guru: *Transcendence for Beginners* is a transformative and transcending experience.'
— Frances Wilson, author of *Electric Spark*

'A book of great intricacy and grace. Clare Carlisle is able to look upon the physics of literature, narrative and being as a scientist might look upon the constellations, giving us both understanding and wonder.'
— Jessica Au, author of *Cold Enough for Snow*

'In this elegant, eloquent, elegiac book, Clare Carlisle describes the movements of other lives, as well as those of her own life, that open paths to understanding what it means to live a life of devotion. This is philosophy as rigorously thought, but also as felt and lived. In an era marked by rampant cruelty and selfishness, *Transcendence for Beginners* offers its readers various modes of the radiant life, one that embraces joy but can also navigate loss and grief in that strange flux of being we call "time."'
— Siri Hustvedt, author of *Mothers, Fathers and Others*

'A wide ranging and surprisingly moving examination of what it is to have, and live, a life.'
— Jessie Greengrass, author of *The High House*

'By taking the discussion on life-writing away from genre towards, instead, philosophical histories of the self, this book makes a powerful case for rethinking life-writing's significance. In the process, it both explores remembering and remembers, doing both with an often startling critical intelligence as well as with surprising emotional immediacy.'
—— Amit Chaudhuri, author of *Sojourn*

'A work of thrilling lucidity and substance, on the singularity of lives and the value of life-writing, in which Clare Carlisle shows herself to be the most companionate of thinkers, gifted with uncommon modesty and intellectual grace. A book to read slowly, talk about, savour and learn from.'
—— Claire Harman, author of *All Sorts of Lives*

'*Transcendence for Beginners* is a brilliant book – one of the most intelligent and sophisticated meditations on life-writing I've ever read, as well as a powerful demonstration of what the best life-writing can do in practice. Carlisle approaches this "humble literary genre" in the fullness of its ethical dimensions.'
—— Edmund Gordon, author of *The Invention of Angela Carter*

Praise for *The Marriage Question*

'*The Marriage Question* already has the stamp of a classic and is bound to enter the canon of great biographies. I was amazed by the clarity of Clare Carlisle's language; she deals with the most complex ideas with miraculous ease. It was a delight to read while at the same time being deeply thought-provoking. I'm already looking forward to reading this magnificent book again.'
—— Celia Paul

'Finally, Eliot has got the biographer she deserves, namely an ardent and eloquent feminist philosopher who shows us how and why Eliot's books, rightly read, are as philosophically profound as any treatise written by a man.'
— Stuart Jeffries, *Observer*

'Clare Carlisle's *The Marriage Question* is the best book I've read on George Eliot.'
— John Carey, *Sunday Times*

'Eloquent and original ... [Carlisle] combines a biographer's eye for stories with a philosopher's nose for questions.... Masterly and enriching.... The ideal historian [of marriage] will need great tact and an impious curiosity. Carlisle has both.'
— James Wood, *New Yorker*

'In this thrilling book, the academic philosopher Clare Carlisle explores the novelist's interrogation of "the double life", meaning not only Eliot's own 25 years of unsanctioned coupledom with Lewes, but also the difficult love relationships she unleashed on her heroines.... Carlisle speaks of wanting to employ biography as philosophical inquiry and here she succeeds magnificently. With great skill and delicacy she has filleted details from Eliot's own life, read closely into her wonderful novels and, most importantly, considered the wider philosophical background in which she was operating.'
— Kathryn Hughes, *Guardian*

'Clare Carlisle brings the work of perhaps our finest English novelist into a brilliant new light.... Following the pulsing and ever-vital questions of love, desire, compromise and companionship, *The Marriage Question* is both a thrilling work on Eliot and a probing, illuminating reflection on modern love.'
— Seán Hewitt, author of *Open, Heaven*

Fitzcarraldo Editions

TRANSCENDENCE
FOR BEGINNERS

LIFE WRITING AND
PHILOSOPHY

*

CLARE CARLISLE

CONTENTS

For little Joseph

Dum curamus eum consequi, et operam damus,
ut intellectum in rectam viam redigamus,
necesse est vivere.

While we pursue this end, and devote ourselves
to bringing the intellect back to the right path,
it is necessary to live.
—— Spinoza, *Treatise on the Emendation of the Intellect*

I. HALFWAY UP A MOUNTAIN

Twenty years ago, before I had a proper job, I met a man who lived in a cave halfway up a mountain in north India. The mountain path began just above Dharamsala, in the foothills of the Himalayas. Under British rule this was an important hill station and the summer residence of at least one Victorian Viceroy of India. Dharamsala's colonial history made it a hospitable place for western travellers. Most days a few tourists hiked to the top of the mountain and back down again. After a couple of hours' walking you reached the cave where this man, whose name I've now forgotten, had a little stall selling bottles of water and soda, snacks and sweets in foil packets, soft chocolate bars, cigarettes.

One day I climbed the mountain with an American woman I'd met at my guest house. On the way back we rested at the stall, looking across the valleys and distant hills stretching out beneath us. The man seemed reserved and rather stern, but in response to our questions he told us that he lived there. Beside the cave was a stone shrine. He called this a temple; it was just large enough for one person to stand inside, with three walls, no door and a roof. When he was sixteen or seventeen he had decided to leave his village down in the valley, renouncing what he'd been taught to hope for: marriage and fatherhood, professional success, a respected place in his community. He had moved into this cave and built his temple. There was no other stall or dwelling along the mountain path and he made enough money to get by. He was now about thirty, a few years older than me. I'd been in India for a couple of months and had seen a lot of sadhus with long matted hair, bare chests and feet, wearing beads and orange dhotis. But this man looked ordinary, in regular trousers, collared shirt and acrylic pullover.

A few days later I walked the path again, this time on my own. I stopped at the stall. The man showed me inside his cave. It was the size of a small room, neat and stark, with a little gas stove, a pan, a cup, a bowl, a bucket. His bed was a piece of cotton laid across the stone floor, and a wool blanket to cover him. It gets very cold up there in the winter. We went back out into the sunshine and sat together watching the great empty sky. He spoke a little English, enough to tell me about stormy nights when the whole mountain raged – 'Boom, full power,' he said, stretching out his arms and opening his eyes wide. There had been times when he thought he was going to die. A few years earlier he had met a European woman, passing along the path like me, and they'd lived together for a while. She stayed a few months, maybe a year. I had the feeling he wanted me to stay with him. An enormous bird of prey flew overhead. How wide was its wingspan, he asked me – surely five feet? – and he stretched out his arms again and said 'Wow, full power!' By this time it was late in the afternoon, the sun was sinking, and if I stayed any longer it would be dark before I reached the town. So I said goodbye and set off down the mountain path, back to my guest house.

My trip to India was coming to an end: in a couple of days I had to fly back to England. The next morning, my last in Dharamsala, I went to a shop that sold Kashmiri shawls and local textiles, and chose some gifts for my family. I also bought two colourful cushion covers embroidered with geometric shapes of trees, animals, birds – one for myself and one for the man in the cave. They came in many colour combinations and I spent ages choosing between them, and more time agonizing about getting one for him, because he might think it was touristy and silly. I bought a soft cushion to go inside his cover and walked back up the mountain path to give it to him. He seemed pleased, and put it in his cave on the stone bed. We sat together again for a couple of hours, smoked some hashish, gazed down into the valley and up into the wide blue sky. He went to get his cushion to look at it again. We tried to figure out what the animal shapes were supposed to be. 'What is this?' he said, pointing to one of them. 'Is it a chicken?' We collapsed laughing, tears filling our eyes.

Then we said goodbye. I walked slowly down the mountain, a little dazed under the bright sun, my heart swelling with something sad and sweet, a feeling I carried with me all the way to Delhi, on the plane to Heathrow, and back home to Manchester. This was my first visit to India and it had changed me. Most intense of all was my feeling for this man, or rather a mixture of feelings, among them an ache of longing – not a longing for him, but a longing we shared, which in his case had found expression in a little temple built stone by stone, with two bare hands, halfway up a mountain. Over the years I've met a few people who exuded a palpable spiritual quality, some rare insight or depth or stillness you could feel in their presence. The man on the mountain was not like that. It was his choice that moved me. This choice seemed full of courage and uncompromising love – but for what? Whenever I thought about it the word 'noble' came to mind, though I puzzled over what exactly that meant.

Eventually these impressions faded until I hardly thought of him at all. After that trip to India I got a job in a university, bought a two-bedroom flat, had a baby. I never went back to Dharamsala and I don't know if he's still there. Then last year I was asked to give the Gifford

17

Lectures at St Andrews and, for reasons I did not immediately understand, I found myself thinking about him
again.

The letter from the Vice-Chancellor explained that
in 1885 Lord Gifford bequeathed to Scotland's finest
universities an endowment for 'Promoting, Advancing,
Teaching and Diffusing the study of "Natural Theology"
in the widest sense of that term, in other words, "the
knowledge of God."' It listed a few of the 'distinguished'
philosophers who had 'delivered' these lectures in the
past: William James, Henri Bergson, Iris Murdoch. This
was surprising, and exciting: something to boast about
for months, even for years... I would have to spend a few
weeks in Fife; maybe rent a house by the sea? My imagination rifled through my wardrobe and swiftly assembled six
lecturing outfits, elegant yet suitable for a Scottish spring.
But there was this annoying part about Natural Theology,
words that conjured rows of thick brown hardbacks
on a dim library shelf, disturbed only by the dwindling
number of students who have to write an essay on the
subject. Each year these books will be thumped onto a
table and scanned for a quote or two; among them William
Paley's *Natural Theology, or Evidences of the Existence
and Attributes of the Deity*, published in 1802, which (the
undergraduate must report) argues that nature is full of
things that have been intelligently, purposefully designed.
Just as a watch can only be made by a skilled watchmaker,
so the universe can only be made by God. Paley, a tal-
ented and admirable man who campaigned vigorously
against the slave trade, is now chiefly remembered for this
watchmaker analogy, which has always struck me as an
uninspiring way to think about both God and nature. Do
we want to imagine ourselves living in a clockwork universe, engineered by a clever God who wound everything

up, then left us to tick along on our own? What kind of religious life can grow under those conditions?

I looked up 'Natural Theology' on the Stanford Encyclopedia of Philosophy, an infallible authority on all sorts of things I ought to know. It was more or less as I'd thought: no longer limited to Paley's effort to argue for the existence of God 'on the basis of observed natural facts', but nevertheless focused on arguments for the existence of God, and definitely avoiding appeals to sacred scriptures or 'mystical experience'. Natural Theology, warns the Stanford Encyclopedia, must 'adhere to the same standards of rational investigation as other philosophical and scientific enterprises, and is subject to the same methods of evaluation and critique.'

Who was Lord Gifford, I wondered, and why did he care so much about Natural Theology that he decided to spend £80,000 – the lion's share of his personal fortune, equivalent to more than £7 million today – to make sure people continued to pursue it?

It turns out that Adam Gifford was a very interesting man, with excellent philosophical taste. Born in Edinburgh in 1820, a few months after Queen Victoria, he did what was expected of a diligent eldest son. He studied Law, established a fine reputation as a defence barrister, and made a lot of money. At work he 'did everything systematically and perfectly'. On Sundays he taught at two Sabbath Schools – a prestigious one for wealthy pupils in the mornings, and a Ragged School for 'poor children' in the afternoons. In 1870, aged fifty, he became a Judge and a Lord. 'It will surprise his friends to know that his heart never was entirely with his profession,' wrote John Gifford, his younger brother.

From his childhood to his deathbed Adam Gifford loved philosophy. He wanted to study 'the highest and

19

most difficult problems of God's nature and man's relation to him'. An invalid for the last few years of his life, he retired to a sunny bedroom, filled it with books, propped himself up on a few feather pillows and immersed himself in reading and writing. 'He spoke freely of what he thought, and most often his thoughts were of God,' recalled his brother. 'He used to say, "God is infinite, how can our finite minds grasp His Being? but it is not wrong to go on in our thinking as far as we can."'

Lord Gifford insisted on intellectual clarity and precision – skills he honed in his legal practice – yet he also liked poetry and panentheism: the view that everything is in God. So it is not surprising that his favourite philosopher was Spinoza. Each one of us is, he believed, 'a part of the Infinite, for the Infinite cannot be infinite if it does not include everything.' Whatever knowledge we can gain of this God 'in whom we live and move and have our being' must come through an effort to know ourselves. These convictions drew him to study Indian philosophy and religion. 'Hinduism or Brahmanism', he learned, 'is a monism, a monotheism and a pantheism of a pure and noble kind.' According to this ancient tradition, all things are in '"Brahm", or "Brahman", (neuter gender)', which is 'neither a person nor a thing, inconceivable and unnameable'.

During the 1870s, before his health declined, Lord Gifford lectured on St Bernard of Clairvaux to the Morningside Literary Institute; on Spinoza's concept of substance to the Edinburgh Young Men's Christian Association; on the avatars of Vishnu to the Granton Literary Society. He explained that *avatar* means descent; that in Hinduism this divine descent may be in any form, not just human form; that belief in incarnations, across different religions, arises from 'the felt possibility, nay the certain truth, that the Infinite can come down, has come down, and is manifest upon earth.' He went all the way to Greenock, forty miles west of Glasgow, to give a very thoughtful talk to the local Philosophical Society on 'Attention as an Instrument of Self Culture', a full seventy years before this now-fashionable subject was claimed by Simone Weil.

Reading the whole of Lord Gifford's will, and not just the bit quoted in the letter from St Andrews, cheered me up even more. While 'Natural Theology' evoked a stiff mixture of rationalism and Christianity – philosophical orthopraxy fused with religious orthodoxy – Gifford was refreshingly open-minded. Lecturers appointed from his bequest must not be subject to any test, made to swear any oath or asked to declare any faith; they could follow 'any religion or way of thinking', or even 'no religion, or they may be so-called sceptics or agnostics or freethinkers.' All he asked was that they were 'sincere lovers of and earnest enquirers after truth.' I liked how he emphasized feeling along with knowing. He wanted his endowed lectures to explore 'the true and felt knowledge (not mere nominal knowledge) of the relations of man and the universe to God, and of the true foundations of all ethics and morals.' And he was willing to wage £80,000 on his belief that 'this knowledge, *when really felt and acted upon*, is the means of our highest well-being.' As with the man on the mountain, this was a choice that moved me.

*

Lord Gifford's endowment expressed his conviction that 'felt knowledge' about our relation to God is not only worth pursuing, but can be shared. This goes to the heart of the ideas I will be putting forward in this book. I want to explore how deep, genuine wisdom and goodness are transmitted by human lives, outside traditional religious structures as well as inside them. Our guide will be Spinoza – not just Lord Gifford's favourite philosopher, but mine as well.

If Gifford's view of Natural Theology was more capacious and holistic than the style of argument exemplified by Paley, this is because he took Spinoza rather than Descartes as his philosophical foundation. The distinction between 'natural' and 'supernatural' knowledge that is still going strong in the Stanford Encyclopedia's article on Natural Theology (last updated in 2020) can be traced to the seventeenth century, when a new generation of philosophers tried to free their thinking from the double bind of church authority and vulgar superstition. They would see things by the purely 'natural light' of reason. For Descartes, their trailblazer, nature was mechanical. God has to be separate from nature; human beings were mechanical bodies animated by free spiritual souls. Paley's clockwork universe is essentially a Cartesian universe, where signs of intelligence in nature point to a supernatural designer. For a Spinozist, however, signs of intelligence in nature are just that: signs of intelligence in nature. They are pointing to what is already here. We are ourselves these signs.

Spinoza was unusual for his time in belonging to no church and claiming no religious affiliation. He was one of his century's most vociferous critics of ecclesial power and superstitious belief. He was also a critic of Descartes: his understanding of nature was rooted in a radically different metaphysics. Whereas Descartes thought we are all individual substances, Spinoza considered us to be 'modes' of the one infinite substance. A substance is whatever exists self-sufficiently, whereas modes depend on something else. The relation of mode to substance is like the relation of a smile to a face, or a wave to the ocean.

In his *Ethics* (1677) Spinoza called the ocean of substance 'God'. Everything that exists, he explained, is in God, and to know it truly is to know its being-in-God. Nothing is outside God or separate from God. We flow from and share in the divine nature, and whenever we act or perceive or think or feel, we are expressing its power. When Spinoza tried to specify our relation to God, these were the verbs he reached for: flowing, sharing (or participating) and expressing.

Spinoza has a reputation for denouncing transcendence. This is thanks in part to Gilles Deleuze, who in 1968 hailed Spinoza as a thinker of 'pure immanence'. By contrasting Spinoza's 'expressionism' with Plato's metaphysics of participation, Deleuze overlooked Spinoza's Neoplatonic tendencies: his debt to the Kabbalah, for example. And by starkly opposing immanence to transcendence – a term Deleuze did not clearly define – he suppressed the variety of possible meanings of transcendence. He seemed to equate it with ontological dualism, and Spinoza's philosophy is certainly non-dualist. Yet if the concept of transcendence posits some boundary, real or apparent, it affirms at the same time a movement that crosses or permeates or breaks this boundary. And if we are thinking of a movement beyond the small self – bounded by its own fears, attachments and defensive patterns of thinking, entrenched by the habit of saying 'I' – then Spinozism, by illuminating and pursuing this movement, is a philosophy of transcendence.

Spinoza's metaphysics suggests that we transcend our habitually circumscribed selves through our interconnectedness with other beings, which can flow into us and change our nature, and also through our connection to God. These movements are a transcendence without dualism, without separation. They are possible precisely because we are all already in God. If we were separate from God, from nature, we would be stranded in ourselves.

Spinoza's conception of a human being is much more dynamic and fluid, its boundaries more porous and provisional, than the everyday notion of selfhood embedded in our grammar, which distinguishes the 'subject' from its own actions and properties as well as from the 'objects' it encounters. This metaphysical selfishness reinforces moral selfishness, and vice versa. Spinoza's non-dualism comes to ethical fruition in his claim that when we truly desire the good, we desire it 'for all human beings', without distinction, including ourselves – and this principle underpins a collective yet nonconformist notion of religion as 'whatever we desire or do, or cause to be done, in virtue of our ... knowing God.'

The *Ethics* is famous for the phrase *Deus sive Natura*, 'God or Nature', which crops up a couple of times in Part IV. This gives rise to an ambiguity: here the word 'Nature' seems to be an alternative name for God, while elsewhere in the text Spinoza uses it to mean the totality of things that are in God. Instead of getting tangled in the denser thickets of Spinoza scholarship, let's just say that while Nature may or may not be distinguishable from God, it is definitely not separate from God. For Spinoza, Nature either *is* God, or *is in* God. This dissolves the distinction between 'natural' and 'supernatural' (or 'revealed') knowledge that underpins the traditional concept of Natural Theology.

Nature as Spinoza conceived it includes the entire field of consciousness, as well as matter, motion, bodies, organic life. It includes feeling, an immediate kind of knowing or awareness. 'We feel, we experience [*sentimus, experimurque*] that we are eternal,' Spinoza wrote in Part V of the *Ethics*. If we want to get some idea of Nature, we can look at, and into, ourselves: these bodies and our consciousness of our bodies; our intelligence, our desire, our fluctuating energies and emotions, our *élan vital* or will to thrive, our capacity to imagine what might be or might have been, our sensitivity and suffering, our creativity, our resilience, our aliveness, our power.

Spinoza was one of the first philosophers to argue that the Jewish and Christian scriptures are human artefacts, shaped by and for the imaginations of a particular community. Nineteenth-century thinkers would coin a new concept to name such a shared world: the 'milieu' or 'environment' – a dynamic ecosystem specific to a place and time that is simultaneously natural, social, intellectual and imagined. The milieu circumscribes the possibilities of what can take root, grow and flourish there. Though Spinoza focused on the Judeo-Christian milieu, his own native habitat, he would no doubt have made the same arguments about the sacred texts, teachings, songs, rituals and art of any other tradition.

For a Spinozist, to say that those traditions are human, and therefore natural, is not to deny that they also express and participate in the divine nature. They could be at once as natural and as divine as the rational and intuitive understanding which Spinoza privileged in the *Ethics* as the surest path to knowing and loving God.

But what about truth? If all our ideas, imaginings, works of art and religious teachings are equally natural, equally in God, does this mean they all have equal truth and value?

Spinoza argued that error consists in a lack of knowledge; more specifically, in mistaking a part for the whole.

Imagine one of those anglepoise desk lamps, bent double to cast a small circle of light on the floor in a dark room. We can see only what is illuminated by that single source of light – a patch of carpet, maybe. The funnel-shaped lampshade keeps most of the room in the dark. If we suppose that nothing exists beyond this small circle of light, we are in error. If we know that we are in fact in a large room, and that when we open the shutters or switch on the ceiling light we will see its walls and furnishings, and notice a person sleeping on a couch in the corner who'll be awakened by the bright light, then we understand that patch of carpet for what it is: a part of a larger whole.

Spinoza titled his masterpiece *Ethica* because he thought the distinction between truth and error matters ethically as well as intellectually. In practice, we are always at least partly in error. Yet the circle of light may grow wider, bring into view more of nature, illuminate more connections between things, encompass a larger portion of the whole.

Doing philosophy means being devoted to this growth and expansion – this Spinozist transcendence. Crucially, the lines between truth and error are not static and ready-made. They must not be drawn according to a doctrinal orthodoxy affirmed by a sacred text or a church, nor by a philosophical tradition – not even Spinozism – received as authoritative. When these orthodoxies funnel the light, they shape a milieu and guide a shared form of life. But they may be a cause of error if we take them to be circumscribing reality as a whole.

This view is, in fact, the distinguishing feature of Natural Theology. It is the common thread running through the Cartesian project carried out by Paley and preserved in the Stanford Encyclopedia, and the wider, Spinozist form of Natural Theology preferred by Lord Gifford.

In the seventeenth century Spinoza's works were banned by the Vatican, denounced by Protestant leaders, and had to be smuggled around Christendom concealed between false covers. About a hundred years after his death his non-dualist, panentheist philosophy – declaring that whatever is, is in God – was finally embraced by three generations of avant-garde German thinkers: Goethe, the Romantics and the Idealists. By the middle of the nineteenth century these ideas were circulating in Britain among freethinking, curious minds of Adam Gifford's generation, above all George Eliot, who made the first English translation of the *Ethics* before channelling Spinozism into her philosophical fiction.

*

The letter from St Andrews arrived when I was three years into a biography of George Eliot, and nearly finished; all paths of thought took me in her direction. I retraced my steps to the cave halfway up a mountain above Dharamsala, which may or may not contain an old embroidered cushion. Twenty years ago, after I said goodbye to the man who lived there, my thoughts turned to his temple again and again. He had made a life stripped to its bare essentials – shelter from sun and storms; a place to sleep; a water source; some fire to cook with; a pan, a cup, a bowl, a bucket; and a shrine: a place dedicated to his God.

I have said that when I tried to make sense of this life, the word 'noble' came to mind – without really knowing what this meant, let alone what it would be for me to learn from his example. Back home I talked to friends about him, hoping someone could explain how he had made me feel. My friend who'd studied Anthropology gave me a stern little lecture on the 'problematic trope' of the noble savage: an uncivilized, morally pure person from some other place or time who lives in simple harmony with nature. When I thought the man in Dharamsala was noble, though, moral purity wasn't what I had in mind. He seemed no less 'civilized' than I was, nor did I imagine that his inner life was any simpler than my own.

Studying the history of philosophy eventually supplied me with an ancient Greek concept, the *kalon*, which came closer to the sense of nobility I'd been reaching for. *To kalon* can be translated as 'what is noble', but also as 'the beautiful' or 'the fine'. For Plato this was a quality of *phenomena*, manifestations; it could be perceived either by our physical senses or with the eyes of our soul. The *kalon* is radiant, glowing, splendid. Its Form is seen 'shining in brightness', just as the Greek poets described their gods as luminous or sparkling. Plato's Socrates teaches that our souls knew the eternal, unchanging Forms before they were incarnated in these bodies – and perhaps we also recognize in some deep buried way this shining quality, which belongs to what is real and true. The *kalon*'s radiance arouses our desire, brings joy and elicits praise. It can be discerned in bodies and objects, in virtuous actions and characters, or in a just political order. Aristotle argued that human happiness consists in living a life devoted to the *kalon*, which Hannah Arendt – the very first woman to give the Gifford Lectures – glossed as 'what is beautiful as opposed to what is necessary and useful'. Saint Paul famously confessed that 'I can will *to kalon* but I cannot do it.'

Whereas goodness, *to agathon*, is relative to specific ends and specific people – something can be good for one purpose and bad for another, or beneficial to one person and harmful to another – the *kalon* simply is noble or beautiful or fine, to anyone with eyes to see it. It was not surprising that I'd felt puzzled by this notion of nobility; one classical scholar describes *to kalon* as an 'enigmatic good', another as an 'unmarked concept'. This concept – or something very close to it – shimmers into view right at the end of Spinoza's *Ethics*, where the difficult and elusive path to beatitude is summarized as *omnia praeclara*: all that is very bright, clear and luminous; very beautiful, splendid and noble.

After being summoned up to Fife to carry out Lord Gifford's wishes and then finding myself recollecting the half-dozen hours I spent sitting on an Indian hillside twenty years ago, I realized that those hours contained all the themes I would want to explore in a series of lectures on Natural Theology. Desire, devotion, courage: themes belonging to a philosophy of the heart. They posed questions about how to be in the world religiously or spiritually (neither word is right) – questions I've thought and written about for years. They evoked a yearning, perhaps a need, for solitude and for companionship, disclosing the choices and sacrifices all that entails. And they made the shape of a story about the power of encountering another human life – how this can touch, move, teach, inspire and form us; draw us in a new direction, or just leave an imprint of longing.

In her recent Gifford Lectures on 'Exemplarist Virtue Theory', Linda Zagzebski considered how supremely admirable people provide models for the rest of us to follow. She chose as her exemplars a 'hero' (Leopold Socha, Holocaust rescuer), a 'saint' (Jean Vanier, founder of L'Arche communities), and a 'sage' (Confucius). In response, the philosopher and psychoanalyst Jonathan Lear argued that even 'very flawed characters' can emit a 'spark of the *kalon*'. He wrote eloquently of his primary

30

school teacher Mr McMahon, a 'local exemplar' who showed him how to live not by modelling exceptional goodness, but by being right there, in his school play-ground. What mattered, for Lear, was the reality of this encounter, and he concluded that it was 'precisely because of his reality that there is much about Mr McMahon that I do not know and could not hope to know... All the aspects of not knowing are part of what it is to experience something real.' Of course, to a ten-year-old boy a school-teacher is an intensely mysterious being. And it is not surprising that a Himalayan hermit remained mysterious to a Mancunian tourist who spent a couple of afternoons in his company. Yet that elusive quality of the real holds true also of exemplars I've now known for more than half my life. These other lives continue to shine with the *kalon* and at the same time I am intrigued by their unseen depth and density, still full of curiosity about them.

For example, I first learned about Spinoza from Susan James, one of my lecturers at university. She stood bravely – it seemed to me – at the front of the classroom and we all watched her speak. Her quietly poised, ele-gant manner seemed to contain a secret simmering joy, somehow transmitting a deep confidence in Spinoza's philosophy. She made it not just accessible but desirable, and habitable. A few years later, when I was twenty-five and trying to finish a PhD on Kierkegaard, I signed up for an eight-week yoga class at the Manchester Buddhist Centre. Christine, the yoga teacher, was both exposed (she was wearing lycra) and enigmatic. She was precise, sensitive, truthful, self-contained, probably in fact a lit-tle shy, and she taught in a way that made us feel she was sharing something she had learned inside herself. She didn't affect a 'spiritual' demeanour, yet she was full of grace. Watching Christine in the yoga studio, trying to follow her movements, gave me one good answer to the Kierkegaard-inspired question that Sheila Heti, meanwhile, was asking in parties and bedrooms and art shows in Toronto: how should a person be? That year I cut my hair short, like Christine's.

Around that time my friend John – whom I'd first met at Susan James's lectures – told me about a meditation retreat he'd just done. He spent ten days sitting in silence, paying attention to his breathing and the sensations in his body from four in the morning to nine in the evening, with five-minute breaks every hour and nothing to eat after midday. It was, he said, life changing. John was a few years older than me and the coolest, cleverest person I knew. Just as I'd copied John by putting sugar in my coffee and stickers on my laptop, so I now signed up for one of those retreats, which was an initiation into new experience and new understanding. For the first time I glimpsed the possibility of observing anxiety, instead of avoiding it or being overwhelmed by it.

Following Christine and John into their practices of yoga and meditation, transmitted from South Asia to the West along routes tracing complicated histories of colonization, conversion and commerce, made me resolve to go to India as soon as possible after finishing my PhD. Without John and Christine I might not have found these spiritual paths. Nor would I have found the mountain path in Dharamsala, and I would be somewhere else today.

I mention these examples not because they are particularly special (though they are of course special to me) but, on the contrary, because they seem typical of how a human life, and perhaps a relation to God, takes shape through encounters with other lives. This phenomenon strikes me as both ordinary and extraordinary. It raises theological questions. The Christian tradition teaches that we relate to God through one unique person, Jesus Christ. In the Hindu tradition God takes many incarnations – such as the ten avatars of Vishnu, the divine sustainer, which Lord Gifford introduced to the members of the Greenock Literary Society, or the multiple manifestations of Śiva, lord of destruction and renewal, to whom, if I remember rightly, that little temple halfway up the mountain was dedicated. In a Spinozist theology, everything is an expression or avatar of God. Everything offers the possibility of divine encounter – but some things more than others. Spinoza thought that God is revealed most clearly and intensely by human minds.

My story of the mountain, the path, the cave, the temple and the man whose choice brought these elements into relation – made them into a home, and into a story – turns out to be rich in archetypes that offer imaginative routes into philosophical themes. In India certain mountains, like certain rivers and trees, are held as especially sacred: these too are incarnations or abodes of God. Then there is Abraham's journey up Mount Moriah, told in the first book of the Hebrew Bible. Kierkegaard seized on this story as a lodestar for his philosophy of religious life. High on the summit of Moriah, half lost in a cloud of unknowing, Abraham must sacrifice his son to God. He must have his heart broken by the pain of human love and loss, must wrestle with doubt and despair, must search for faith in fear and trembling.

My man is halfway up his mountain, rather than at its peak – yet while Abraham walked right to the top of Moriah and then came down again, back to his people on the plains, this man went halfway up and lived there, inside the mountain. He became, for me, a living parable of being-in-God.

The path, also, is a generative symbol for a life. Paths symbolize transmission as well as quest. A path is a tradition, a way through the world that has been carved and cultivated by those who have gone before, sustained by repetition. We bequeath it to future generations as we walk along it. Following a path means following other people (or maybe beings of other kinds), whether we actually see them on the path ahead of us or whether this path exists at all only because they once made, sustained and renewed it. If we look over our shoulder, we may realize that we too are being followed. Following – a complex act that encompasses desire, imitation, discipleship, faith, devotion – gives human lives their unique shapes, while linking them together.

The cave, meanwhile, evokes a primal scene of western philosophy. Plato, probably still the greatest storyteller in this tradition, described how Socrates asked his students to imagine they were prisoners trapped inside a dark underground cave, entranced by shadows on the wall. They devise games, competitions, tournaments, to see who is best at recognizing the shadows and predicting their movements. This cave is at once a shelter and a prison: an ambiguous symbol of the world, or of our own minds. Another time, Socrates's students were told to picture themselves swimming in murky waters at the bottom of the ocean. Both scenarios portray the philosopher's task as learning to breathe in the open air, in touch with what is real. On this view, philosophy is akin to certain strands of religious practice, and also to modern therapeutic techniques. It is oriented to ideals of awakening, enlightenment and liberation.

Not long after I returned from that first trip to India, I saw Jonathan Lear give a lecture on Plato's cave. He interpreted it as a sort of guided meditation that allows people to see and feel the distinction between how things appear and what they truly are. Socrates used this exercise to change his students' souls and reorder their desires – to convert them to philosophy, the pursuit of wisdom. And in a way, Lear's lecture helped convert me to philosophy. Plato's cave became vivid not simply as a familiar passage from a famous book, perhaps an analogy or a parable, but as an imaginative experience – and not a private, incommunicable experience, but one that might be transmitted and shared. This crystallized a question that was bothering me: what is the connection between philosophy and life? Pessimism about this question had made me disinclined to pursue an academic career. That day though, in the lecture hall, I swung towards optimism and decided to make an effort to get a job in a university. But the question still bothers me. Philosophy, the love of wisdom, is an ideal at once unarguable and radically open-ended – because we cannot assume we know what wisdom is, or how to acquire it; because what passes for wisdom, indeed for philosophy itself, might just be shadows on the wall.

Plato describes the cave in a way that emphasizes the difficulty of climbing out of it. The cave in India, however, was open to the hillside and the sunlight. The little temple, too, had just three walls and a roof, open to the elements. If my story was a dream and I wanted to interpret it, I would be tempted to see those images of mountain, path, open cave, open temple, open sky, as invitations to leave behind what I've been taught and envisage a new kind of Natural Theology. Except of course it isn't new – it's as old as the hills. I might discern in the dream a desire to situate theology in a nature that is elemental, mineral, vegetal, animal, divine – a shared nature, of which our human lives, resplendent with thought and creativity, are a part and an expression.

If this is a desire, it is also a question. Questions are the avatars of philosophy's desire: the shapes through which we enter into relation to the truth we're seeking. What would it mean to do philosophy or theology in the open air, halfway up the mountain, somewhere in the middle of our lives? Not necessarily to demolish or abandon classrooms, universities, libraries, but to envision these structures with just three walls, and a roof for shelter from the storms. And maybe a couple of embroidered cushions – something that bespeaks care, art, beauty, intimacy, and renders our austere conceptual spaces more habitable. In my Gifford Lectures, I decided, life stories would make a home for philosophy. I could start with the Indian man in the cave, and then I would talk about Lord Gifford – an unlikely pair, seemingly worlds apart, which my own life, and probably my life only, had brought together and turned into a story.

II. LIFE WRITING

Biography is a humble literary genre, rooted in our natural curiosity about other people. This desire to know
already carries the seed of a philosophical quest that arises, according to Plato, in the gap between appearances
and reality. I meet someone, see how she presents herself – and then I wonder, what's she really like? What is
she not telling or showing me? But while Socrates went
around Athens asking, 'What is a human being?', I want
to know *who* this singular person is.

A biography's subject matter is typically a whole life.
One whole human life, from birth to death – that's a
lot. Not just a lot of time, but a lot happening. And, for
a philosopher, a lot to think about. This subject has special ethical weight: people often say that a human life is
precious, even sacred. According to Aristotle, ethics is
concerned with whole lives, because happiness or flourishing 'requires a complete life'. If you believe in God,
you might imagine how he will judge your life as a whole,
once it is finished. So the concept of a whole life is on the
horizon of ethics, and on the horizon, I think, of our day-
to-day experience. This concept seems ready and waiting
to spring into thoughts like, What am I doing with my
life? or, Oh my God I'm at least halfway through my life.

Yet being on the horizon also means that it is elusive. It
is very hard, if not impossible, to pick out the entity captured by the concept of one whole life. Right now, for each
of us, our whole life is a mystery. Perhaps biographies,
like fictional life stories, appeal to such a wide reading
public because they offer the chance to move at lightning
speed through a life that has clearer contours than our
own, and thereby gain some sense of a wholeness that
usually eludes us – a metaphysical impulse, spurred on

by love of gossip. Moreover, and this troubles a philosopher, the very concept of a life is difficult to pin down. It seems somewhat different from adjacent concepts such as person, individual or self – unless you think, like Leibniz, that the concept of a person includes everything that has happened and will ever happen to him, as well as all the ways he was, is and will be connected to other things, so that each human soul contains 'traces of everything that happens in the universe, even though God alone could recognise them all.'

The practice of life writing brings into view this concept of a whole life. Of course, a biographer need not enter directly into metaphysical speculations. Rather, in grappling with technical and aesthetic questions that arise while writing a life – questions about literary form, authorial judgment, narrative voice – she draws closer to the question of the *being* of a life. Truth becomes especially salient. Another person's *whole life* is a weighty subject: even if the biographer does not appoint herself as its judge, she is making it available for public judgement. So her account must be truthful and fair. But what does that entail?

This question was posed by André Maurois, biographer of Shelley, Byron, Voltaire, George Sand, Balzac and Proust, when he gave the Clark Lectures at Trinity College, Cambridge about a hundred years ago. His theme was biography considered as both an art and a science. He urged that a life must be written 'with a strict care for the truth – a care not only for the truths of fact (so far as the unfortunate biographer can attain them) but for that profounder truth which is poetic truth.' As Maurois discovered, life writing turns out to be a rather elastic genre in which distinctions between fact and imagination, between description and interpretation, between fiction and non-fiction, are not easily drawn. In the effort to choose words that minimize the constant risk of lapsing into untruth, the biographer runs into the deep question of the truth of a life.

That, at least, was my experience – and it seems to have been Maurois's too, given his tenacity and his difficulty in pinning down the nature of biographical truth. My first biography ended with these two sentences:

> Following Kierkegaard through his final months to his last days in Frederiks Hospital, I sensed the mysterious weight of a human life, glimpsed in its entirety. It is elusive and intimate, slight and immense, fragile and astonishing.

My biography of George Eliot likewise ended by invoking her life-as-a-whole:

> Perhaps a biographer's devotion is a little like the devotion of a spouse. Writing a person's life means living with them intimately, struggling to understand them, wondering how far they can be trusted, dealing with the ways they resist, annoy, disappoint, challenge and elude you. It means staying with them for their whole life, if not for your own – though such a close encounter with another person is bound to leave you changed, even as you move on.

This repetition between my two conclusions, written several years apart, was not planned. I've only just noticed it. But I don't think it's a coincidence. It happened because life writing brings into view the concept – and the question – of a whole life.

Bio-graphy, life writing, is by definition a literary encounter with a life. It is an ancient art, and still going strong. Is writing in some special way appropriate to a life

– this entity that, whatever it may be, however elusive, certainly has a singular shape or form?

Consider this childhood memory. When I was a little girl, before I started school, my mother taught me to write. First I learned to write the alphabet with a pencil on lined paper. Letters were a mixture of curved and straight lines. An 'a' was quite difficult: you began to draw a circle – but you didn't make it a whole circle – and then you put a straight vertical line on the right-hand side of it. 'b' was a tall letter, made from a circle and a vertical line twice the height of the 'a', on the left side. When I wrote my name, I had to draw a 'C' as tall as a 'b'. The lined paper helped me get the proportions right. My mother's writing was round, clear, flowing, very beautiful. She could join all the letters in each word together. I tried to make my letters more beautiful, like hers. I tried hard not to make any mistakes.

At some point in primary school the daily act of writing became so habitual that I no longer thought about it. Even as a philosophy student and, eventually, a professional philosopher, I hardly paused to wonder, what is writing? What are we doing when we write?

Recollecting the experience of learning to write helps to lift this veil of habit. When I bring my attention back to writing, I discover that in some ways it resembles life. Writing a text means drawing a certain line on a page; living a life means drawing a certain line through the world. These lines move through space and through time.

A path seems a fitting metaphor for writing as well as for life. In each case you must find or make a path through terrain that is teeming with possibilities. And yet the path of writing, like the path of life, can quickly acquire a trajectory that feels irresistible, even necessary. Often your path is formed by following others who have gone before you. Sometimes it is formed by choices – a decision to go

40

this way, not that way. Every path is a combination of following and choosing, and choosing whom to follow, and following others' choices. Every path is some combination of finding and making.

Life is relational, and so is writing. It is the relationships between words, and then between sentences, that make a meaningful text. And in writing as in life, linearity combines with complexity. On the one hand, the line of writing is unidirectional. It only moves forwards. On the other hand – yet at the same time – it loops, folds, gathers, knots, stitches itself together, forming layers. For example, a recurring metaphor, a rhyme, or a repeated word tacks one point in the line to another. Life shares this double character. It flows irrevocably in one direction: sooner or later (it's taken me many years) we learn that we cannot travel back in time. Yet our experience continually folds back and loops forward – in memory, in habit, in the deliberate repetitions of practice and ritual, in all the moods of anticipation, and in all the moods of looking back.

The line of writing, like the line of living, has an intermittent and rhythmic quality. On paper there are spaces between words; in our bodies there are spaces between breaths, between heartbeats, between footsteps. In consciousness there are longer intermittencies of sleeping and waking, and irregular intermittencies as attention lapses and returns. Underlying these stops and starts is a flow, such as the flow of blood through the body, and the flow of thought – unconscious as well as conscious – that underlies the act of writing. A piece of writing, like a living being, has rhythm, and its rhythm is essential to its structure (how it moves) and its texture (how it feels).

Inseparable from this rhythm is temporality. As soon as a text comes into being it is there all at once on the page. Yet writing and reading are active, imaginative experiences that unfold in time, bringing the text to life and sustaining it in existence – just as a footpath through the countryside is formed and renewed by each person or animal who walks along it. Likewise, we can distinguish these two aspects of a human life: it is a dynamic shape unfolding moment by moment, and it can be conceived as a whole. Then it transcends the flow of time. Indeed, this is an image *of* time, like an aerial view of a great river from its source to the sea, seen from miles above the earth – 'under the aspect of eternity', as Spinoza put it. When we imagine it this way, it becomes quite beautiful. A whole life, moving through the world from its source to its end: unique, slender, searching. A God looking down on it may well be moved to love – and also, perhaps, to tears.

*

In her memoir *Out of Africa*, Karen Blixen recalls a story she was told as a child. Now she titles it 'The Roads of Life'. A man is awakened in the night by a terrible noise. He goes outside to investigate, running up and down in the dark, stumbling and falling into ditches, listening for the source of the noise. Eventually he finds a leaky dike, sets to work plugging the leak, then goes back to bed. When daylight comes, he sees how his footsteps traced the shape of a stork in the muddy ground. 'I am glad that I have been told this story and will remember it in the hour of need,' writes Blixen. 'The tight place, the pit in which I am now lying – of what bird is it the talon? When the design of my life is completed, shall I, shall others see a stork?'

Adriana Cavarero cites this story at the beginning of her book *Relating Narratives: Storytelling and Selfhood*,

When I was a child I was shown a picture,—a kind of moving picture inasmuch as it was created before your eyes and while the artist was telling the story of it. This story was told, every time, in the same words.

In a little round house with a round window and a little triangular garden in front there lived a   man. Not far from the house there was a   pond with a lot of fish in it.

One night the man was woken up by a terrible noise, and set out in the dark to find the cause of it. He took the road to the pond.

Here the story-teller began to draw, as upon a map of the movements of an army, a plan of the roads taken by the man.

He first ran to the South. Here he stumbled   over a big stone in the middle of the road, and a little   farther he fell into a ditch, got up, fell into a   ditch, got up, fell into a third ditch, and got out   of that.

Then he saw that he had been mistaken,   and ran back to the North. But here again the noise   seemed to him to come from the South, and he   a g a i n ran back there. He first stumbled over   a big stone in the middle of the road, then a little   later he fell into a ditch, got up, fell into another ditch, got up, fell into a third ditch, and got out of that.

He now distinctly heard that   the noise came from the end of the pond. He   rushed to the place, and saw that a big leakage had   been made in the dam, and the water was running   out with all the fishes in it. He set to work and   stopped the hole, and only   when this had   b e e n done did he go   back to bed.

When now the   next morning the man looked out of his   little round window,— thus the tale was   finished, as dramatically as possible,—what   did he see?— A stork!

I am glad that I have   been told this story and I will remember it   in the hour of need.

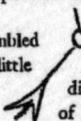

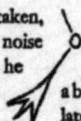

which inspired Elena Ferrante's Neapolitan novels – narrated by Elena Greco, a feminist literary scholar whose research interests resemble Cavarero's. The man's nocturnal adventure, Cavarero explains, symbolizes a whole life: only afterwards, seen from the outside or from above, does its shape come into view. She draws from this parable the lesson that we cannot tell our own life story.

Here Cavarero echoes Hannah Arendt, who argued that

> the "who", which appears so clearly and unmistakably to others, remains hidden from the person himself, like the daimon in Greek religion which accompanies each man throughout his life, always looking over his shoulder from behind and thus visible only to those he encounters.

Arendt developed this thought in her Gifford Lectures, delivered in Aberdeen in the early '70s and later published in *The Life of the Mind*. She talked about the distinction between appearance and reality that is dramatized in Plato's cave, and has run through the philosophical tradition ever since. Appearing, she said, constitutes the unity of a life.

> To be alive means to live in a world that preceded one's own arrival and will survive one's departure. On this level of sheer being alive, appearance and disappearance, as they follow upon each other, are the primordial events, which as such mark out time, the time span between birth and death.

Cavarero cites Arendt when she argues that 'for millennia, philosophy has diverted its gaze from the appearance of human beings because it cannot tolerate their most scandalous property, their realness, together with their contingency.' She depicts life writing as insurgent against philosophy, because it examines the unique singularity of a life. Philosophy seeks general definitions – What is man? – whereas the biographer asks, Who is this man? or, Who is this woman? (Cavarero insists that the 'Who?' question is always gendered.) 'Unlike philosophy, which ... has persisted in capturing the universal in the trap of definition, narration reveals the finite in its fragile uniqueness, and sings its glory,' writes Cavarero.

I'm also drawn to this romantic view, though I don't entirely trust it. What if narration does not sing a life's glory, but exposes its secrets, highlights its pettiness and compromises, or distorts its truth? And can the narrator avoid appropriating that life for her own ends?

Answering the more speculative question of the relationship between philosophy and biography will depend, of course, on your conception of philosophy. You might turn to life writing for a feminist critique of a patriarchal tradition, if you agree with Cavarero (and Ferrante) that interest in one another's stories is a particularly feminine trait. Or, on the contrary, you might conceive life writing as philosophy's handmaiden. In her 2003 Gifford Lectures, Eleonore Stump argued that narratives – especially biblical narratives – can enrich our understanding of suffering. Stump, a Catholic philosopher, distinguished between propositional 'Dominican' knowledge, exemplified by the rigorous analytical reasoning of Thomas Aquinas, and interpersonal 'Franciscan' knowledge, which is immediate and intuitive. Franciscan knowing can arise in two different situations: second-person encounters (that just means meeting someone and getting to know them), and literary narratives. Biography fits squarely into Stump's category of Franciscan knowledge since it involves both situations:

over time a biographer encounters her subject, then facilitates the reader's encounter with this person via a written narrative. Stump portrayed Franciscan knowledge as a helpful assistant – a soft pliable handmaiden – to rigorous Dominican knowledge. 'Narratives are an aid to thinking through certain philosophical issues,' she explained, 'not a rival to philosophy itself.' While she turned to narrative to expand academic philosophy beyond its rather narrow borders, she reinforced those borders by maintaining a clear distinction between a personal, intuitive kind of knowing and 'philosophy itself'.

Both Cavarero and Stump bring narrative and philosophy together; they also emphasize, for very different reasons, how they diverge: life writing rebelliously contests philosophy, or submits to its imperious demands. But what if we saw life writing as full of philosophical potential? This might even stretch our ideas about what philosophy is and how it should be done. Wittgenstein's biographer Ray Monk has argued that biography can (and should) carry out the work of philosophy as Wittgenstein conceived it: to look rather than think; to describe rather than explain; to 'see connections'. Monk thinks that 'the biographer's duty, like that of Wittgenstein's philosopher, is to resist the "craving for generality" characteristic of those who aspire to science.' In other words, he agrees with Cavarero that biography is concerned with the singular as opposed to the general – yet he believes that philosophy, properly practiced, shares precisely this concern.

While these are valuable thoughts, they leave untouched deeper questions about the being of the biographical subject and the nature of biographical encounters. These questions concern us all because biography only brings into sharper focus a concept of life-as-a-whole that already hovers on the horizon of our experience, glowing with ethical and existential significance.

When Aristotle argues that human flourishing requires a complete life, he combines – or maybe slides between – two normative notions of 'complete': the quantitative completeness of ending in old age, having passed through all the phases of life; and a qualitative completeness comprising a range of intellectual, familial, social and civic accomplishments. A vaguer notion of normative completeness shows up in the existentialists' ideal of authenticity, most conspicuously in Heidegger's *Being and Time*. 'We all feel our real life to be a deformation of our possible life,' declared the existentialist writer José Ortega y Gasset in a 1932 essay on Goethe and biography. Ortega linked 'the mystery of the authentic I which lies behind our actual life' to concepts of 'destiny' and 'vocation' – and he argued that the biographer's task is to 'weigh the subject's fidelity to ... his possible life' in order to 'determine the degree of authenticity of his actual life'.

I don't share this view of the biographer's task, and I don't like it. The murky concept of a life-as-a-whole that emerged from my own biographical work is purely descriptive, not normative or aspirational. Speaking descriptively, it does not make sense to say that some people live a whole or full life, and others do not – if, for example, they die young or never fulfil their potential. Any person's life, from birth to death – no matter how long or short it was, no matter what it accomplished or left undone – is by definition a whole life. And it is their actual life, not some other life that might have been. You may of course feel that your actual life falls short of what it could be or should be – or other people might make this judgement about you. But all those ideas and thoughts and feelings are part of your actual life: features of its experience, and aspects of its meaning. The biographer's task is to uncover that life, in its actuality and its inwardness; in its self-understanding and its multiple appearances in the eyes of others.

What would it mean to succeed at this task? By the time I'd finished writing my biography of Kierkegaard, I was at least asking myself this question. Then someone told me to read Etienne Souriau's *The Different Modes of Existence*. At the end of the book was the text of a lecture Souriau gave in Paris in 1956 on 'The mode of existence of the work to-be-made (*l'oeuvre à faire*).' Like his existentialist contemporaries, Souriau argued that we ourselves – like everything that exists – are works to be made: we are metaphysically unfinished, incomplete, under construction, in a process of becoming. Yet this thought drew from the Greek concept of *poesis*: a making that is not pure creativity, but the uncovering of some reality which, we might even say, desires to be and to be seen. Could our life-as-a-whole be like this? Souriau emphasized that a work-to-be-made is essentially elusive, just as a horizon is elusive. However – and this was the point of his lecture – the experience of creative activity, such as writing a book or making a piece of art or constructing a philosophical argument, gives us some insight into the elusive, work-to-be-made quality of our own existence.

Souriau described how a work-to-be-made – let's say, a book to be written – exists for the writer in a manner that is 'enigmatic and remote, yet intense'. Insistent and exacting, it pursues its author and demands her attention. 'The work's call is a bit like the call of the child who wakes his deeply sleeping mother. She is immediately aware that he needs her.' Yes: any book or essay I write absorbs me, whether I like it or not; it nags me until I finish it, distracts me from other tasks, pulls my attention from my loved ones, prevents me from resting – it does indeed wake me up in the night to minister to some sentence or paragraph, or stops me sleeping in the first place. In the creative process, Souriau suggested, we encounter first-hand the work-to-be-made: this mysterious entity that shares our own being. We experience its passage from virtuality to concreteness – a passage that always involves 'a measure of failure', even if it also brings a sense of accomplishment, perhaps exaltation.

'Everyone knows the work's call,' wrote Souriau, 'because everyone has had to answer to it. It awakens us at night to make us feel the time passing by, the severely limited time that remains to us for all that remains for us to do.' Here he touches on an experience I've had repeatedly: how writing a book (like raising a child) confronts me with my mortality, haunts me with the fear that I might not live long enough to finish it – and then fills me with relief when it turns out that there was indeed enough time, that my life is longer and larger than it might have been.

Souriau's lecture brought into view two aspects of biographical practice: the searching, demanding work of writing, and the compelling yet elusive entity that is one whole, complete human life – not our own life, in this case, but someone else's. The biographer's literary labour in pursuit of that life offers a chance of encountering this entity and enquiring into its being – even in the inevitable failure to grasp it.

A whole life is transcendent – beyond experience, exceeding all appearances – yet the biographer is responding to its call. That call has ethical weight. No one is morally obliged to write a life, and indeed doing so without the subject's authorization, as must happen with any historical biography, may be morally dubious. But having undertaken the task, the writer should carry it out with as much truthfulness and justice as she can muster. At the same time, this biographical encounter involves creativity, perhaps artistic freedom. Just as the life's path through the world took shape through a combination of finding and making, so in the biographer's attempt to follow this path their own poetic work of imagining and interpreting becomes entwined with the work of discovery and verification.

It's a familiar thought that the truth of a life-as-a-whole – which the biographer pursues and which strikes each of us, I imagine, with wonder – exists as an idea in the mind of God. That was Leibniz's view, and Spinoza meant something similar when he talked about the truth of finite things *sub specie aeternitatis*: a whole life, a temporal entity, unfolded, so to speak, in God, where it is known as a whole. Some philosophers of religion have construed God's omniscience in quantitative terms: the mind of God, like an Akashic record or a super surveillance computer, contains all the truths that exist, of which we know just a few bits and pieces. More than this, though – and here we can only speculate – wouldn't God, seeing all the truths about a life, also see them differently, perhaps transformatively, through loving, forgiving eyes? And would God see something metaphysical that must elude even an omniscient biographer (let's hypothesize one, for a moment): not just every detail of a life, but the journey of a soul?

People who once came very close to death have said they saw their whole life flash before them: all of it, yet in an instant – a flash! – as if they were finally seeing themselves in God, and through God's eyes.

These ideas continue to be expressed in ritual commemorations of lives that have passed away. Once a person dies, their whole life is invoked at the funeral, under the banner of its name and circumscribed by the dates of its birth and death. Someone might say that the life is 'laid to rest', as if it were all stretched out before them. None of the mourners has had access to this whole life. Yet the collective gathering of witnesses to some of its different aspects and phases approximates and symbolizes its wholeness. The life's story, from cradle to grave, will be told in an extremely abridged form – a miniature biography, recited in just a few minutes. This ritual of witness-bearing and storytelling traditionally takes place before a God who *does* see and know the whole life. The mourners' shared task is to carry the mystery that is (or was) this life and offer it to God – as if they were delivering a parcel, not knowing what's inside. And God, if he is there, receives it.

*

As Cavarero says, echoing Arendt, a human life has an exhibitive, expressive quality: it shows itself in the world. This is why the ancient Greeks included human lives among the things they called *kalon*: the quality of radiant beauty or nobility that belongs only to things that appear. And biography is only possible because lives leave traces of their appearance. The biographer gathers up these traces and turns them into a story, narrates them as a whole in order to bring into view the life's arc, from beginning to end, which seems so hard to grasp or even to glimpse from the inside. This is the artistic or aesthetic element of biography: uncovering a life's shape, and perhaps its *kalon* qualities.

I've tried to describe how a line of writing can follow and reveal – with some mixture of creativity and discovery – the line of a life. But there are counterpoints to this claim. It is hard to disagree when Arendt points out that a life appears at birth and disappears at death; yet the meantime, stretching between these 'primordial events', is a continual dance of appearing and disappearing. Yes, human lives tend to exhibit themselves; they are, nevertheless, always partially hidden. It may even be that the most significant truths about a life – its deepest meanings – are guarded and dissembled. Kierkegaard had strong views about 'inwardness': this kernel of the human self, the site of its relationship to God, was, he insisted, inaccessible to other people. True, that insistence was both an ardent 'yes' to God and a petulant 'no' to everyone who'd disappointed him; it voiced both his yearning to be understood and his dread of exposure. But still he felt that who he was before God – an 'eternal consciousness' – was utterly different from the awkward, intense, contradictory man who appeared in the eyes of the world. As his biographer, I found myself seeking Kierkegaard's inner truth while contending with his own claim that this was an impossible task.

There is also, of course, the more prosaic and happenstance fact that much will be missing from any biography. It is rare to gain access to another person's quotidian experience: the flow of faces, atmospheres and tones of voice that once filled their subjectivity. According to Proust, we access our own past experiences of this type only by accident, in involuntary memory. Annie Ernaux evokes such things in *Exteriors*, a record of scraps of suburban life that only underscores how much goes unrecorded of 'an existence' which Ernaux elsewhere describes as 'singular but also merged with the movements of a generation'. Most lives are mostly undocumented; some documents that once existed may have been lost or destroyed, or even buried, like George Eliot's love letters. The biographer must select from the sources that remain – make a path through the material, as I said. A biography is not an exhaustive chronicle. Nor should it be, for aesthetic reasons: ironically, an excess of detail can thwart the attempt to grasp a life in its wholeness and reveal its singular shape.

Finally, life's diffusive quality is a counterpoint to its relentless linear arc. At the end of *Middlemarch*, George Eliot sums up the life of her heroine, Dorothea, by noting that 'the effect of her being on those around her was incalculably diffusive'. Actually Eliot is telling us that Dorothea's life cannot be summed up: it is incalculable. We detect in these words Eliot's critique of Utilitarianism, an approach to ethics that depends on the calculation of effects. The novel as a whole dramatizes the Spinozist principle that everything is interconnected, not just historically but metaphysically. Each individual being is at once porous and self-transcending, constituted by its effects on others as well as by the effects of others on itself. And Dorothea's effects will not be gathered up. No one can measure their significance, or bind them into a whole.

Surely this holds true of every life. Its diffuseness is not at all at odds with its singularity: each life makes a unique pattern of diffusions. But we cannot trace this pattern, just as we can't trace the part of a wave that soaks into the sand before it withdraws into the sea. Even the word 'part' feels inappropriately precise here. To know a whole life, we would have to know both the innumerable influences it has absorbed and its own reverberations – and this is impossible.

'Diffuse' can mean two things: spreading over a large area, and lacking clarity or definition. Diffusion is not the same as fragmentation or incompleteness. A diffuse life is whole, but its wholeness is elusive (at least to human knowers). A work of biography might be begun, but in a certain sense it can never be concluded. Eliot – not a biographer, but certainly a philosophical life-writer – seems to have grappled with this fact. When she reflected on the difficulty of ending a novel, she may have been thinking of the difficulty of completing the story of a life. She concluded *Middlemarch* with a gesture of both revelation and concealment, appearance and disappearance. Here are those closing sentences in full:

> Her finely-touched spirit had still its fine issues, though they were not widely visible. Her full nature, like that river of which Cyrus broke the strength, spent itself in channels which had no great name on earth. But the effect of her being on those around her was incalculably diffusive: for the growing good of the world is partly dependent on unhistoric acts; and that things are not so ill with you and me as they might have been, is half owing to the number who lived faithfully a hidden life, and rest in unvisited tombs.

Dorothea has added goodness to the world, though it is impossible to say exactly how. Her acts are not widely visible, unhistoric, undocumented, and they end in doubled obscurity – an unvisited tomb. Her life is literally hidden away, buried underground. All that endures is an incalculable, indeed unverifiable, truth: that some other lives are not so bad as they might have been.

Eliot is here playing very delicately with an ethic of exemplarity – a Spinozist way of thinking about human goodness that contrasts with the Utilitarian and Kantian ethics ascendant during her own lifetime. *Middlemarch* began with a classic moral exemplar, Theresa of Avila, who reappears in its penultimate paragraph: the question of exemplarity is clearly in view. What moral theorists now call 'exemplarism' differs from an ethics structured according to principles, rules or maxims, in the tradition of Kant and Mill. As Gandhi argued against the British Utilitarians who governed India, moral concepts such as law, imperative and obligation generate a rhetoric of violation and transgression, of blame and criticism, that fosters violence. By contrast, exemplarity gives rise to disappointment – the great theme of *Middlemarch* – and also to hope, the counterpart of disappointment.

In order to be exemplary, an action or a life must be visible to others. Moral exemplarity used to be regarded as the chief purpose of biography, from the gospels and lives of saints to its modern incarnations. 'However difficult biography may be', André Maurois declared at the end of his Clark Lectures,

> it merits the devotion of our toil and of our emotions.
> The cult of the hero is as old as mankind. It sets before men examples which are lofty but not inaccessible, astonishing but not incredible, and it is this double quality which makes it the most convincing of art-forms and the most human of religions.

In her Gifford Lectures, Hannah Arendt pointed out that the Greeks called heroes '*andres epiphanies*, men who are fully manifest'. And in *Fear and Trembling* – a book about the problematic idea that Abraham should be followed as an exemplar – Kierkegaard notes that even a celebrated 'hero' such as Abraham needs his 'poet' to keep him visible in the world. Poets are exceptionally sensitive to beauty, in the holistic sense conveyed by the Greek *kalon*, and exceptionally skilled at transmitting this beauty in writing. Unless poets tell compelling life stories, exemplars will fade from view and eventually be forgotten. Kierkegaard's reflections on the hero and the poet evoke pairings such as Socrates and his poet Plato, Jesus and the gospel writers, as well as that most troubling hero, Abraham, and Kierkegaard, his troubled poet.

The nineteenth century was dominated by notions of 'great men', epitomized by Carlyle's *On Heroes, Hero-Worship, and the Heroic in History* (1841), Comte's positivist calendar (1849) and Emerson's *Representative Men* (1850). 'Their spirit diffuses itself,' wrote Emerson: 'this is the key to the power of the greatest men.' These ideas pressed upon Eliot during her twenties, a period of intense philosophical apprenticeship. Carlyle, Comte and Emerson were all formative influences for her, though eventually she would smash their patriarchal ideal. While Nietzsche, for all his iconoclastic hammering, left this ideal intact and fitted his own life and work to its mould, *Middlemarch* subverts it in a double way: by contemplating a female hero, Saint Theresa, and by refracting her exemplarity through Dorothea's unhistoric life. This was not just an aesthetic choice – to 'cut herself off', as a contemporary critic put it, 'from the splendid effects of Scott, from the stately beauties of Thackeray, from the thrilling horror of Balzac and Dickens.' Eliot's dedication to ordinariness had a moral urgency, and especially for women. 'See how diffusive your one little life may be,' she counselled her younger friend Jane Senior, who felt crushed by the narrowness of married life. Human goodness, she added, was 'the only guarantee that there can be any other sort of goodness in the universe.' Eliot believed, like Spinoza – and in stark contrast to Nietzsche – that the best exemplars are not elite, exceptional heroes but, on the contrary, those who embody a good that can be shared by all.

Both Eliot and Kierkegaard put life writing to philosophical use and stretched the boundaries of modern philosophy in the process. While neither were biographers or autobiographers in any conventional sense, they took singular human lives, considered in their temporal narrative flow, as the subject of philosophical enquiry. Both were hyper-attentive to inner experience. Interestingly, marriage – such a decisive feature of a life's narrative arc – lies at the heart of their work, a bubbling source of existential questions. Eliot's close attention to 'real life' reflected her belief that art's purpose lay in transmitting the good, the true and the beautiful, just as Kierkegaard's experiments in literary style expressed his existentialist principles. Inspired by Ruskin's 'realism' – 'the doctrine that all truth and beauty are to be attained by a humble and faithful study of nature' – Eliot thought literature that rendered a life's emotional truth could move readers to deeper sympathy in their real-life encounters and relationships.

Above all, Eliot was interested in the moral power of ordinary lives, like Dorothea's, whose effects are 'not widely visible', though nevertheless 'diffuse'. Such lives can be rendered visible by art. Some feminist readers have criticized Eliot for depicting obscure wives and mothers, such as Dorothea, rather than allowing her heroines to have extraordinary lives like her own. I see this as a philosophical decision, rooted in a radical (and Spinozist) ethic of exemplarity and committed to exploring the disappointment and the hope this entails. Eliot was a poet of mediocrity, a gospel writer of hidden lives. Writing Dorothea's story rescues her from oblivion and bears witness to the fact that the world is better, more beautiful – more *kalon* – for this one rather unremarkable life having moved through it. Similarly, we are better for having read the book. The qualities of beauty and goodness discerned in Dorothea's life also shine in the words chosen to convey the significance of that life. Just as a life leaves it trace, having passed through the world, so a book leaves its trace in us. Something slender yet diffuse, incalculable, has passed through our own inner life.

Those closing lines of *Middlemarch*, now among the most famous passages in English literature, seem to be about two things at once: life and writing. The way Dorothea's river-like 'full nature' has flowed into finer 'channels' suggests the flow of ink from a pen into fine lines; these flows have carried feeling, particularly yearning and determination. Eliot is reflecting on Dorothea's life as a whole and also on her own poetic search for the beauty, truth and goodness of a human life.

Is this the aim of all writing? Is it the arc of life itself? I am reminded again of being three or four years old, pencil in hand, trying to get my letters right – trying to make them look nice, trying to copy my mother. Looking back I see a child striving for beauty, truth and goodness, before she knew how to write the words.

III. THE MILIEU

Whether we are considering biography or the experiments in 'life' literature carried out by Kierkegaard or George Eliot or Proust, philosophy and art converge in life writing. But are philosophy and art really two different things that may – or may not – come together? Here we have to distinguish between philosophical questions and the practice, discipline or method we've come to call 'philosophy'. Questions about truth, goodness and beauty; freedom, desire and suffering; time, memory and selfhood; life's meaning and purpose, are accessible to all. In fact it can be difficult to avoid them even if we try. Many artists explore and wrestle with these philosophical questions in their work.

Yet philosophical practice is not the same as artistic practice, and this is true whether we have in mind the broad, holistic philosophy exemplified by thinkers such as Descartes and Spinoza, or the more specialized philosophy now done in universities. Philosophers differ from artists not simply because they use different tools and techniques, discipline their attention in different ways, and work within different institutions, but because they have a different kind of task. Artists are makers. Whether they create objects, texts, music, performances or encounters, 'making' is the verb artists most often use to describe their practice. Philosophers make things too, of course. They construct arguments, invent examples and thought experiments, write books; Deleuze even claimed that philosophy consists in creating concepts. But if they are seldom heard to say that they are 'making' philosophy, this is because their creativity is typically a means to another end. That end is the removal of whatever conceals, distorts or gets in the way of truth.

Through history, philosophers have repeatedly described themselves as clearing away prejudices, superstitions, errors, confusions, illusions, ideologies, ambiguities, pseudo-problems and 'fictions' (concepts that don't correspond to anything real). Influential philosophers in both Indian and European traditions have conceived their work as therapeutic. Like physicians, they are getting rid of disease: reverting to an original condition, not creating something new. Or, to vary the metaphor, they are housekeeping: clearing out cupboards, tidying drawers, sweeping floors, cleaning windows, unblocking sinks, taking out the trash. Heidegger famously wrote that language is 'the house of being' – and philosophers want to keep that house in order.

The ancient Greek word *kosmos*, meaning order, arrangement or adornment, had a quotidian sense, like setting a table for dinner, or it could be applied to the whole universe. In the *Timaeus*, Plato portrays philosophy as cosmic exegesis. Putting things in order renders them more intelligible, and also more beautiful. Notice that this phrase, 'putting things in order', leaves open a question on which philosophers, unsurprisingly, disagree. Are we restoring order, putting things *back* to some pre-existent, prelapsarian logos or law? Or are we imposing an improvised, contingent order on pure flux or emptiness?

The artistic part of us hopes to bring something new and singular into the world; the philosophical part of us wants to declutter it. In making, artists 'explore'; in tidying up and sorting out, philosophers 'argue'. I've drawn these distinctions not to keep art and philosophy apart, but, on the contrary, to understand better how they are combined. Philosophy today is highly disciplined and can be set in its ways; yet it is still fundamentally in formation.

When reading or writing philosophy, literary style is for me as open to question as the metaphysical or epistemic assumptions that we philosophers pride ourselves on testing. An author's search for the right voice and form – inseparable of course from seeking the right words – can yield as close an encounter with truth as searching for the best argument.

In the last chapter I asked how the art of life writing both succeeds and fails in revealing a whole, singular life. My question now is, what does a life reveal? Does it just express itself – or something beyond itself?

Spinoza believed that a philosopher must consider things in their relations to a larger whole. After declaring that 'whatever is, is in God', he emphasized that every being is 'part of Nature'. From these exceedingly general statements, he built a bridge to the possibility of knowing singular things (finite modes) by asserting that we know a thing by knowing its causes. Spinoza's metaphysics gives this claim a double meaning. First, the immanent cause of each thing is God or Nature. Second, it is also true to say that every finite thing depends on a complex network of other finite things. While this network extends eventually to comprise the whole of Nature, the local circle of causes supporting each thing is more particular. A coral living on the bed of the ocean has its own habitat, different from that of an owl in the woods. Every being is a singular centre of a world – and I imagine each world as a series of eccentric spheres, expanding outwards until the sphere becomes unfathomably large: the cosmos as a whole.

I've said that a path is a good metaphor for a human life, with its linear form, moving from a first moment to a last; its momentum and trajectory; its combined qualities of forging and following. But this metaphor is less successful in capturing how a life expresses a world.

Casting our eyes beyond the path, to the right and left, we notice plants growing, from delicate flowers to towering trees. Any one of these living beings, with its roots reaching down beneath the ground and its leaves stretching towards the sky, will exemplify Spinoza's thought about the dependence and interconnectedness of all things. Each plant manifests the nature of the seed that generated it, the composition of its soil, a changing climate, the cycle of seasons, a certain configuration of water, air, heat, light. Its life is inseparable from, and expressive of, its world.

Plants, of course, do not move themselves from one location to another – they do not carve paths through the world in this sense – and they were traditionally classified as a lower life-form than animals. Yet plants accomplish astonishing transformations within a single year: from seed to stem, flower, leaf, fruit. Their visible form reveals a natural capacity for radical change that is also found in human lives. It was for this reason that Goethe, set on developing a holistic science of life, wrote a treatise on *The Metamorphosis of Plants*.

Goethe published this treatise in 1790. Over the next fifty years in Germany, France, England, the new science of biology crystallized around a new concept: the milieu. This concept drew attention to the relations between a living thing and its surrounding conditions of existence. The German noun was *Umwelt*, the 'around world'; English provided both 'circumstances' and 'environment'. But the French *milieu*, signifying 'middle' as well as 'around', was perfect. In his 1952 essay 'Le vivant et son milieu', the philosopher of science Georges Canguilhem declared that this concept had become 'a basic category of contemporary thought'; 'a universal and obligatory means of registering the experience and existence of living things'. Tracing its evolution over the first decades of the nineteenth century, he noted how Lamarck's *les circonstances* and Etienne Geoffroy Saint-Hilaire's *le milieu ambiant* preceded Auguste Comte's use of *le milieu* in 1838, evoking 'a certain intuition of a centred formation'.

If a life is a line, limited by a beginning and end, a milieu is a sphere and a surrounding. Lines and spheres are geometric figures, but – like the continually unfurling line of a life – a milieu is temporal and dynamic. It can change very radically indeed; think of climate change and historical change. Then there is the maternal milieu: the 'baby-and-mother cosmos' explored by the psychoanalyst Hans Loewald, who combined Freudian theory with the philosophy of Heidegger, his former teacher. Every human life begins in the middle of its mother's body and must endure a traumatic passage from this totalizing, undifferentiated milieu to a world in which maternal care fluctuates, and mixes with many influences and atmospheres. This transition is paradigmatically ambiguous. It facilitates physical, emotional and intellectual growth; perhaps the growth of a soul. It is also an experience of rupture and loss. Most cultures contain vivid emblems of the maternal milieu – Gaia, Parvati, Mary, for example – which express its overwhelming power, and also its elusiveness, its inwardness, its mystery.

Canguilhem, with his focus on modern science, ignored these feminine archetypes, though his essay on the milieu emphasizes that the concept can accommodate quite different ontologies – from mechanistic to organicist philosophies of nature, for example. The milieu also accommodates different relationship dynamics between individual things and their surroundings. Some scientists, explained Canguilhem, considered individuals to be determined by their milieu, while others proposed a more constructive or reciprocal relation between self and world. Mid-nineteenth-century biology developed through a clash between Lamarckians, who saw the milieu as 'indifferent' to the needs of organisms which tried to adapt to it, and Darwinians, for whom an organism's primary milieu was populated by 'enemies or allies, prey or predators', foregrounding relationships of 'use, destruction and defence'. Canguilhem himself was drawn to the holistic theory of life developed by the neurologist Kurt Goldstein while in exile from Nazi Germany. For Goldstein, the relationship between a living being and its 'continuously forming' milieu is like a dialogue. In pathological cases this becomes a violent argument – a relation of struggle or confrontation – whereas a healthy life is 'almost gentle in its flexibility'.

Human beings can, of course, be studied as an animal species within a biological milieu. But during the middle years of the nineteenth century the new science of 'sociology' emerged in tandem with developments in biology. Here the concept of milieu was stretched to encompass cultural as well as natural conditions of life. In the early 1850s the English philosopher Herbert Spencer read Comte's *Cours de philosophie positive* at the urging of George Eliot – at that time plain Marian Evans, in love with Spencer and about to have her heart broken by him. Spencer developed Comte's concept of milieu, proposing 'environment' as a single term naming biological and social circumstances. He hypothesized that living things are constantly adjusting to their environment. His *Principles of Psychology* set out to analyse both physical and mental relations 'between every organism and the external world' – anticipating the theory of adaptation soon to be presented in Darwin's *Origin of Species*.

In France, meanwhile, Balzac's equally ambitious attempt to depict different 'social species' in a series of realist novels followed the lead of biologists such as Cuvier and Saint-Hilaire. In the preface to his life's work, the *Comédie humaine*, Balzac argued that society resembles nature – 'For does not society modify Man, according to the conditions [*les milieux*] in which he lives and acts, into men as manifold as the species in Zoology?' Human beings, Balzac suggested, shape their milieu as they are shaped by it – and this reciprocal poesis produces an intellectual, imaginative world. 'Man has a tendency to express [*à représenter*] his culture, his thoughts, and his life in everything he appropriates to his use,' Balzac wrote in 1842.

Art not only expresses and adorns a milieu, but illuminates and even transfigures it. Proust believed that Balzac's readers 'came to see a sort of literary quality in a hundred everyday occurrences.' After he recreated his own milieu in his immense novel *In Search of Lost Time* he wrote that 'reading enhances the value of life, a value we have not realised until books make us aware of how great that value is.' Or here is Eve Babitz, another transfiguring author, explaining how C. P. Snow's 'air of lucidity is just so strong it permeates your whole life while you're reading him so that you don't make any false moves', and how Reynar Banham's *Los Angeles: The Architecture of Four Ecologies* 'can make you see beauty where you only saw ugliness before.' Babitz herself was an artist-devotee of LA milieux, though by then (the '60s and '70s) people called them scenes. Back in France, her contemporary Annie Ernaux was plotting her own Proustian search-and-rescue: 'in her book she would like to save everything that has continually been around her. She wants to save her *circumstance*... She will go within herself only to retrieve the world.'

Each milieu is a world both singular and shared. It

comprises the surroundings relative to, and configured by, a singular life. The maternal milieu exemplifies this singularity: there is nothing general about *my* mother. Yet the milieu is at the same time a complex web of multiple relations, an ecosystem, a community, 'a common time'.

*

If each living thing is, by definition, in the middle of its milieu, then no two milieux are identical – but nor are they entirely separate. Two plants growing next to one another have virtually the same milieu: the same soil, the same sky, the same seasons. The cultural and psychological elements of the human milieu, which Balzac and Spencer began to analyse in the nineteenth century, mean that spatial proximity both is and is not a guarantor of a shared milieu. Imagine the different families living on a London street, 'of all faiths and none' as Anglican priests like to say in a special cosy voice. In some respects their milieux coincide: they enjoy or endure the same weather, walk through the same streets and parks, use the same transport system, send their children to the same school, live under the same laws. Yet they inhabit different imaginative worlds, different cosmologies. They may think differently about the meaning of a human life.

This cosmological dimension of our milieux is often described as a worldview: some picture of the cosmos as a whole. Implicit here is a certain conception of self, world and the relationship between them: a sense of ourselves as self-contained subjectivities set apart from the world, and thus able to have a 'view' or 'picture' of it, rather than porous beings immersed in the world. It belongs, in other words, within an ontological framework that is more Cartesian than Spinozist. Better to say that each human being inhabits a milieu with cosmic dimensions, in addition to (and indeed inseparable from) its biological, social, cultural and historical dimensions. Some general understanding of what exists and how things relate to one another is sewn into our milieux, sometimes implicitly, sometimes explicitly, like a running stitch that appears and disappears through the fabric.

This idea is crystallized in John Tresch's concept of a cosmogram – the same John who encouraged me to try meditation back in the '90s. A cosmogram is a particular thing, such as an object or a myth or a dance, that offers an image of the cosmos as a whole. At the same time, it embodies and articulates its specific milieu: the materials it was made from, the crafts and technologies used to produce it, the ways it is (or was) engaged with or put to use.

The concept of a cosmogram can itself be used in at least two different ways. It can pick out certain artefacts – such as a Hindu temple, a world atlas, a Chinese garden or an icon of a pregnant Mary – which have the special feature of invoking a cosmic totality. Or the concept can be applied to any object as a hermeneutic lens, provoking us to interpret it cosmogrammatically – it could be a shopping trolley, or a photo of avocado toast on Instagram, or a pair of trainers. What worlds do these objects and images disclose? Heidegger asked this question of Van Gogh's painting of a pair of old boots; his answer – like his choice of image – was drenched in nostalgia and tainted with horrible politics, but the question still stands. And this example shows how our own imaginative work collaborates with objects to make them into cosmograms.

If we ask how a particular human life expresses a milieu with cosmological dimensions, we are preparing to read it cosmogrammatically. Life writing then turns out to be a cosmological art. With some difficult-to-parse mixture of revealing and rendering, biography discloses a life as a shape – unfolds it as an image or a narrative arc – so that it becomes readable in this way.

It can be dazzling to think that there are multiple cosmological milieux, none of them verifiable by criteria or methods which are not themselves part of that milieu, or of some other milieu. This thought – call it pluralism – continues to resist my efforts to think it through. It seems to me that the experience of inhabiting a cosmos has a certain modality: this is one possible world among others. Its possibility and its plausibility are linked to the practical fact that it is indeed habitable, liveable. It is viable, in the literal sense of being able to make your way through it. Yet a possible world can be inhabited with various and fluctuating degrees of conviction. Some individuals or groups may never entertain or imagine alternatives to their milieu. Or someone might inhabit the milieu of, say, secularism and modern science, yet wonder if there is 'something more' – some 'spiritual' reality – 'beyond it'. Another person might, conversely, inhabit a traditional religious cosmology, yet doubt its truth, with this doubt taking shape in the spectre of an atheist, materialist world. Perhaps it is a peculiarly modern experience to flit from one cosmos to another, or to feel unsure which world you're living in – or perhaps people have always felt this way. I imagine these worlds as spherical structures with a certain density: a very dense milieu shuts out alternative cosmic possibilities, and is occupied with a high degree of certainty, whereas a more translucent milieu lets in the light of other possible worlds. Lighter is not straightforwardly preferable to darker, nor vice versa, though sometimes I envy people whose world seems more solid than my own shifting, diaphanous cosmos.

So we can notice different textures of cosmological

consciousness, as well as different cosmic structures. Writing my biographies of Kierkegaard and George Eliot, I discovered in both lives a metaphysical texture woven from an intense experience of vocation, providence, destiny – a kind of spiritual necessity – and an equally intense experience of contingency. Kierkegaard theorized this texture when he argued that a human self is a synthesis of necessity and possibility. He likened possibility to oxygen; without it, we feel 'unable to breathe', spiritually suffocated. What Kierkegaard called possibility, Eliot called 'an imagined otherwise': a vivid awareness of how one's past, present or future might be different. 'I sometimes wonder what my life had been / Without that voice as channel to my soul,' says the heroine of *Armgart* – a middle-aged artist who, like her author, worries that her best work may be behind her. Eliot wrote this poem in 1870, full of doubts about the new novel, *Middlemarch*, that she was trying to bring into being. Perhaps Kierkegaard and Eliot were so alive to possibility, and its mysterious interactions with what is or becomes necessary, because they spent so much of their time writing. Their daily work, pen in hand, was to carve a path through possibilities, to turn this way, not that way. Eliot once described this literary process as a passage to 'the irrevocable'.

Contemplating the milieu's cosmic and metaphysical dimensions, the two questions I tried to hold apart in the last chapter – the Socratic question, what is a human being? and the biographical question, who is this person? – seem to become entwined. When we imagine lives unfolding in milieux that include certain ideas or assumptions about human beings and their relation to the cosmos, then we find 'what?' questions inscribed within 'who?' questions.

A singular life expresses its milieu as it expresses itself. And when biography reveals or recreates a human life as a whole, it also reveals or recreates the world in which that life took shape – a world that must be both similar to and different from our own.

This was the view of Wilhelm Dilthey, who published the first volume of a biography of Friedrich Schleiermacher in 1870 – as Eliot was struggling with the early chapters of *Middlemarch*. Dilthey was influenced by Goethe and Schleiermacher and, through them, by a Spinozist pantheism. Writing biographies was part of his effort to develop a philosophy of life, rooted in experience. Though he never completed his *Life of Schleiermacher*, he wrote biographical studies of Leibniz, Goethe, Schiller and Hegel, among others. Dilthey's interest in the way a human life expresses its entire world must have been inspired by Leibniz's metaphysical vision of souls as living cosmograms: 'living mirrors or images of the universe'.

Unlike Leibniz, though, Dilthey rejected the idea that our paths unfold according to a divine plan. Embracing a Romantic awe of human creativity, he explored how we find and make patterns out of our own lives, in the process of living. While autobiography depicts this meaning-making with a 'special intimacy of understanding', a biographer, Dilthey argued, has the privilege of seeing the whole of a life and discerning patterns of influence and action which never became fully conscious for the individual in question. Writing a biography, he discovered, involved reassembling the subject's 'life-world'. Understanding Schleiermacher meant seeing the interconnections of German mysticism and pietism, Lutheran Protestantism, the philosophy of Spinoza, the poetry of Lessing, Goethe and Schiller, the intellectual climate in Berlin at the turn of the nineteenth century. This milieu shaped Schleiermacher's life, and this particular life discloses the milieu. Echoing Carlyle's 'heroes' and Emerson's 'representative men', Dilthey used the phrase 'significant individual' to describe how a single life embodies a historical moment or milieu. In 1887, reflecting on his first work of biography two decades earlier, he explained that he had 'wanted to investigate how, in the laboratory of a significant mind like Schleiermacher, totally disparate elements of culture coalesce into a whole and react back on life'. Jean-Paul Sartre – whose biographies of Baudelaire, Genet and Flaubert make bold philosophical arguments – repeated this idea in the 1960s, first in an essay on Kierkegaard titled 'The Singular Universal', and then in his sprawling study of Flaubert. 'A human being carries a whole epoch within him, just as a wave carries the whole of the sea,' wrote Sartre.

*

Great intellectuals – and by this we tend to mean great readers and writers – are like funnels that draw in entire traditions and bring them to singular expression. This is certainly true of George Eliot, whose life's milieu, stretching exactly across the middle of her century, was woven from all those strands which Dilthey gathered into his *Life of Schleiermacher*, as well as from Romanticism itself and the philosophies of Hegel and Feuerbach that had followed it; from Comte's positivism, and the new evolutionary and social sciences pioneered by Darwin and Spencer; from English traditions of myth and poetry; from histories of Judaism and Christianity; from an English landscape dramatically reshaped, during her lifetime, by the ambiguous 'progress' of industry; from the complex machinations of Britain's imperial policies in India, Africa and North America; from legal reforms that gave new rights to working men, to women, to Jews and Catholics; from a dawning consciousness of patriarchy. The concept of milieu itself emerged as Eliot grew as a thinker and writer in the 1840s and '50s, and then she put it to work in her fiction.

The title she chose for *Middlemarch* hints at a milieu, and a path, that unfolds through history. This novel dramatizes a world at once biological, social and poetic. It is populated by legends of saints, by histories of art and science, and by the ancient mythologies which its doomed scholar, Edward Casaubon, tries in vain to synthesize; at the same time it is galvanized by the forward march of politics and technology, according to narratives of progress and reform. The novel brings to light how this milieu forms the lives of its interconnected characters. In Eliot's hands, though, the concept of milieu – Canguilhem's 'centred formation' – merges with a different thought: the human ego's world-making, pictured as 'a lighted candle as a centre of illumination' that is placed against a mirror covered in 'minute and multitudinous' scratches. These tiny scratches stand for 'events' which, seen by the flame of self, 'will seem to arrange themselves in a fine series of concentric circles round that little sun'.

This 'parable' of self-centring formation mirrors not just ordinary human egotism, but also the artist's creative work. In both cases, subjectivity rays out and arranges a world. What is form in art, asked Eliot, 'but a set of relations selected and combined in accordance with the sequence of mental states in the constructor, or with the preconception of the whole which he has inwardly evolved?' When young Maggie Tulliver daydreams, 'refashioning her little world into just what she should like it to be', she both repeats and – if she resembles Eliot as a child – anticipates her author's literary world-making.

Like many of her contemporaries, Eliot was interested in how people make a home in the world: how they adapt, or fail to adapt, to their conditions of existence. Ambitious Dr Lydgate, for example, finds that 'the petty medium of Middlemarch' is 'too strong for him'. More distinctive in her work is her attention to the maternal milieu that remains the original home of every human life. The world as George Eliot should like it to be is a world seen through the eyes of a loving mother, infused with gentle acceptance, never 'hard and unkind' or punitive – quite different from the world envisioned in patriarchal religion, and from Eliot's own inner world.

Eliot's experience of being mothered was paradigmatic, though perhaps unusually intense. When she was still a baby her mother, Christiana Evans, became pregnant with twin boys, who both died in infancy. Eliot's mother went through pregnancy, labour and grief during the first months of Eliot's life, and after losing her twins she seems to have withdrawn from her three remaining children, sending them first to a local childminder, then away to school. Eliot, the youngest, went to boarding school at the age of five. When she was sixteen her mother died, probably of breast cancer.

As I wrote Eliot's life, Christiana Evans came into view as an absence more than a presence – a powerful, influential absence. This maternal figure cast a long shadow, stretching through her daughter's life in the shape of a longing for love, a deep well of grief, and a keen sense of both the joys and the pains of emotional attachment. Eliot's inner world was filled with anxiety and longing, pervaded by an uneasy 'sense of what was not', as she put it in her autobiographical poem 'Self and Life'. Written in middle age, this dialogue reckons with the loss of her maternal milieu:

LIFE.

I was thy warmth upon thy mother's knee
When light and life within her eyes were one
...
Was it person? Was it thing?
Was it touch or whispering?
It was bliss and it was I:
Bliss was what thou knew'st me by.

SELF.

Soon I knew thee more by Fear
And sense of what was not,
Haunting all I held most dear;
I had a double lot:
Ardour, cheated with alloy,
Wept the more for dreams of joy.

This personal loss had a cultural counterpart. Eliot was born into a world stripped of maternal icons. When Roman Christianity had colonized Britain, images of the Virgin Mary replaced native mother-goddesses; after the Protestant reformation, these Marian images were themselves destroyed.

It is easy to critique the way the Catholic Church curated Mary's image. With this emblem of virginal, submissive motherhood, men circumscribed women's power. The doctrine of the immaculate conception, declared an infallible tenet of faith in 1854, underscored Mary's difference from all other women: apart from this mythical Mary, no woman could bring into being something divine. Yet Mary somehow outshines the church that tried to contain her – and that church, to its credit, has preserved beautiful liturgies and artworks through which she shines upon new lives. She remains a potent symbol of the maternal milieu, reminding us of the physical, psychological and spiritual source of every human life. She gives us permission to feel and show our longing for this source. She is beautiful, but not in a sexually available way, and this innocent beauty, seen as if through a child's eyes, connects us to the experience of being a child – an experience that stubbornly persists inside us, in some secret or shadowy way, as we grow older. Looking at Mary, we become children again.

Given these entangled personal and cultural histories, it is not surprising that Eliot was moved by the Madonna and Child paintings she saw during trips to Germany and Italy in the 1850s and '60s. She was following in the footsteps of the feminist art historian Anna Jameson, author of a series of books on sacred art, including *Legends of the Madonna* (1852). For Jameson, Mary embodied 'the union of the divine and the human in feminine form' – a bold unorthodox thought; she inspired 'hope in a higher as well as a gentler power than that of the strong hand and the might that makes the right'. This Mary disrupted patriarchal power even as she submitted to it. And Eliot learned from Jameson to see Mary as an archetype infused with pre-Christian ideas of a mother goddess, harbouring multiple meanings and close to the natural world. Iconographies of Mary connected her with the sun, the moon, the star of the sea. She was both the lily, symbol of purity, and the rose, symbol of love and beauty; both a fragrant cedar tree, exalted for its healing powers, and an olive tree, the sign of peace, hope and abundance. Mary is an organizing image in *Silas Marner* and *Romola*, written soon after Eliot's first trip to Italy. In both novels Mary transmits the fantasy of a pure-hearted, utterly loving mother which hides in its shadow an experience of maternal ambivalence that Eliot knew first-hand.

Maybe this maternal archetype resonates with Eliot's distinctive image of multiple worlds, nested within one another. *The Mill on the Floss*, her most autobiographical novel, compels the reader to move back and forth between its characters' narrow provincial world and the wide milieu of a sophisticated narrator steeped in classical literature, the history of Christianity, Romantic art. This literary device replicates Eliot's own experience of moving between these two worlds – an experience that had a tragic aspect. While she worked on this second novel, her siblings had cut ties with her after learning that she was 'living in sin' with her partner, George Lewes. This painful loss, rendering her unable to return to the world that had once been home, repeated her early loss of her mother.

Eliot made the idea of worlds within worlds a principle of literary form. Like *The Mill on the Floss*, *Middlemarch* is a 'study of provincial life': the subtitle echoes Balzac's *Scènes de la vie de province*, yet Eliot situates this small world within a wider geographical horizon. New philosophies and scientific theories flow into Middlemarch from European cities, while troublesome young men are shipped off to the colonies. In a direct address to the reader, Eliot explains that she has deliberately curtailed the novel's milieu. Her task of understanding a few singular lives has, she suggests, confined her attention to their immediate surroundings:

> I at least have so much to do in unravelling certain human
> lots and seeing how they were woven and interwoven, that

all the light I can command must be concentrated on this particular web, and not dispersed over that tempting range of relevancies called the universe.

This remark is not without irony, since *Middlemarch* is about much more than Middlemarch; here Eliot invokes a cosmic milieu – 'the universe' – in the very act of pushing it beyond the periphery of her narrative gaze.

At the core of this novel is the relationship between what is ordinary and trivial, and what is great and significant. Fantasizing about marrying her scholarly neighbour Edward Casaubon, young Dorothea dreams of greatness: 'There would be nothing trivial about our lives. Every-day things with us would mean the greatest things. It would be like marrying Pascal... I should see how it was possible to live a grand life here – now – in England.' Here the irony is doubled. Its first moment is tragicomic, because we already suspect – and Dorothea is soon to discover – that Casaubon is a very petty person. But then a new twist: Dorothea's life story *is* grand as well as trivial. While Saint Theresa's life was a paradigm of remarkable goodness, Dorothea exemplifies an inconspicuous, 'unhistoric' goodness that both augments and reveals the goodness of the world.

This was also an unfolding theme in Eliot's life. The life named 'Mary Ann Evans', a young woman sunk in provincial obscurity, flowed into a life named 'George Eliot', who fits Dilthey's description of a 'significant individual'. Returning to Italy in the mid-1860s, now a celebrated novelist, Eliot perceived this narrative arc in Titian's 'Annunciation': here was a young woman 'chosen to fulfil a great destiny, entailing a terribly different experience from that of ordinary womanhood'. Was Eliot trying to make sense of her own life? Looking back on her childhood, she now recalled how 'ardour's magic sense / Made poor things rich to thee and small things great.'

In her final novel, *Daniel Deronda*, she developed the aesthetic principle of concentric (and eccentric) worlds to its fullest expression. Here the action unfolds in an explicitly cosmic milieu: human beings are compared to planets, and the narrator to an astronomer. Eliot prepared to write *Daniel Deronda* by surrounding herself with towers of books on Jewish history and theology; she became particularly interested in the Kabbalah. This Neoplatonic Jewish tradition teaches that the source of all things is an unknowable, indescribable God, named in Hebrew *En-Soph*, meaning 'no end', or *Ohr En Soph*, 'endless light'. All souls were born from this divine source, and long to return to it – just as the human souls in Plato's *Timaeus* long to return to their native star. If a soul becomes isolated, too weak to travel alone, it 'chooses a companion soul of better fortune and more strength', which becomes 'the mother', carrying and nurturing the weaker soul to help it on its journey back to God.

Like an infinite sun, Eliot learned, the *En-Soph* 'rays out' ten manifestations called *Sefiroth*. Her notes describe this emanation as 'a spiritual substance or force or medium', bringing in the concept of milieu (which she often translated as 'medium') to help her imagine the *Sefiroth* as a series of metaphysical spheres. The ten *Sefiroth* create countless worlds: ours is one among many. 'Individuals in the lower world,' Eliot wrote in her notebook one day in 1874, 'have their types in the higher, so that nothing here is trivial, but all has a higher significance... Especially is the human soul a complete citizen of the higher world & stands in immediate connection with all the Sephiroth.' Another day, she jotted down a Talmudic proverb: 'A man's life is like the shadow of a bird that flies.'

In the *Daniel Deronda* notebook these grand cosmological ideas are juxtaposed with passages from Fontenelle's *Entretiens sur la pluralité des mondes* (1686), a poetic work of popular physics exploring the post-Copernican experience of feeling 'lost amongst millions of worlds'. Fontenelle's narrator, a man of science, takes night walks with a beautiful woman. Together they look up at the starry sky and contemplate their place in an 'unbounded' universe. She feels bewildered by the thought that 'every fixed sun is a star, which diffuses light to its surrounding worlds'; she wonders if her brief life on this one small earth means anything at all. Yet their conversations end on a happy, if wistful note. 'I am acquainted with the whole system of the universe! how learned I am!' exclaims the lady on their last walk. 'Yes,' replies her companion, 'I only ask as a reward for my trouble, that whenever you see the sun, the skies, the stars, you think of me.' You can see why Eliot enjoyed this seventeenth-century text, with its blend of astronomy, romance and existential questioning. *Daniel Deronda* tacks between the modern scientific universe invoked by Fontenelle, and the Kabbalistic cosmos; its characters, whether they know it or not, inhabit both constellations of worlds.

The milieu summoned in *Daniel Deronda* contains a vision of what transcends it. It is not simply a web complexly woven out of biological and social tissues, but a world within worlds. This novel enacts a literary argument; each singular life unfolds within, and is shaped by, a cosmological milieu – and each life radiates, in its own unique unfolding, a divine source of truth, beauty and goodness.

Inspired by her own experiments with the form of the novel, Eliot thought beyond the biological, social and cultural conceptions of milieu that preoccupied Darwin,

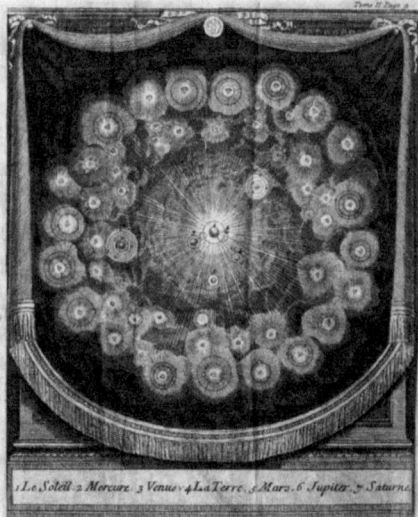

1 Le Soleil. 2 Mercure. 3 Venus. 4 La Terre. 5 Mars. 6 Jupiter. 7 Saturne.

ENTRETIENS

SUR

LA PLURALITÉ

DES MONDES.

A MONSIEUR L...

V OUS voulez, Monſieur, que je vous rende un compte exact de la manière dont j'ai paſſé mon temps à la campagne, chez Madame la Marquiſe de G***. Savez-vous bien que ce compte exact ſera un Livre, & ce qu'il y a de pis, un Livre de Philoſophie? Vous vous attendez à des Fêtes, à des Parties de Jeu ou de Chaſſe, & vous aurez des Planètes, des Mondes, des Tourbillons; il n'a

Spencer, Comte and Balzac. She came to see individual lives expressing a whole in ways at once more poetic, more feminine, more Spinozist, more cosmic. And while Dilthey focused on significant individuals, Eliot proposed that every human life is in truth much larger than it seems. 'Your one little life' contains untold histories, epic journeys, magnificent hopes, grand passions, immense struggles and profound losses.

IV. INCARNATIONS

A couple of years ago, while I was writing my biography of George Eliot, I passed the age my mother was when she died. In the spring of 1994 she was diagnosed with a terminal illness, and she died on 1 May the following year, a few days before her forty-fifth birthday. My mother did not follow any religion, and during that last year of her life certain questions – spiritual questions, let's say – became pressing. Her GP, a stern elderly lady doctor who had a special liking for her, took her to church a few times, but she didn't find what she was searching for. Instead she got in her old Mini and drove up to the Isle of Skye. It was a long way, nine or ten hours' drive from our Manchester suburb. She stayed in a little white house high above the sea on the island's north-west coast. At the end of the long summer between A-levels and university I went there with my father to scatter her ashes, and the couple who owned the house told me she used to spend hours sitting on the hillside, looking out to sea. Among her notebooks I found some writing she'd done on Skye. Somehow I managed to lose those notebooks, and I only remember one line: 'If I had a life before, then it was here.'

As I turned forty-five, then forty-six, I felt myself no longer following in my mother's footsteps, but going on ahead of her. It was strange to think of her as a younger woman – someone who might learn from me. At the same time, writing about George Eliot gave me a sense of returning home, to something she and I shared, after I'd ventured far away from her experience by going to Cambridge, studying philosophy, meeting so many different sorts of people, practising yoga and meditation, travelling to India, eventually – improbably – becoming a philosophy professor. My mother loved books, but she'd left school at sixteen and married young. In her thirties, once my sister and I were at school, she went to evening classes to take A-levels in English Literature and Sociology. She left Britain twice in her life, for holidays in France and Spain. She worked part-time at the local hospital, booking appointments. She was seen mainly as a daughter, a wife and a mother. She probably never heard of Kierkegaard or Spinoza or any of the philosophers I discovered at university a few months after she died. But one or two of George Eliot's novels were on the bookcase in our house. Now I was returning to those novels with everything I had learned over twenty-five years – and finding that much of it was already there.

My mother was the sort of person for whom Lord Gifford endowed his lectures on Natural Theology. He taught evening classes and Sunday-school classes, and he wanted the Gifford Lectures to be 'public and popular, open ... to the whole community ... whether receiving University instruction or not.' When I think of my mother sitting on that hillside, looking out to sea, considering her life and her death, wondering where her soul had been – and, I imagine, where it might be going – I ask myself if I have anything to teach her. And when I say 'her', I also mean anyone: the part of us that is simply human, living on this earth beneath a blue or clouded sky, with some time to wonder: Who am I?

*

The claim that Jesus Christ is 'the Incarnation' and 'only son' of God, rooted deep in Christianized cultures, carries with it certain ideas about a human life. Casting Jesus as the sole incarnation casts all others as witnesses and potential beneficiaries – as perceivers and receivers

83

of a divine gift. The most pertinent spiritual question to ask of each person becomes: how well or badly have they received this revelation? And if they do believe in Jesus as the son of God, how constantly and wholeheartedly have they lived out their faith?

These questions structure the narrative drama of the gospels. Who is Jesus? And who recognizes him, who rejects him? This is a drama of the one and the many. Here is the one incarnation and there are the multitudes, the crowds, which are subdivided into the followers of Christ and everyone else.

I am not going to advocate for one crowd or the other, and anyway I don't quite know how to place myself between them. Instead I want to think about the under-lying logic of the one and the many that structured the very concept of incarnation in the world I grew up in. Not that I personally had a Christian upbringing: this logic had survived the decline of faith, and maybe it contrib-uted to that decline. It cast the many – in other words, all of us – as perceivers rather than bearers of truth. We were not encouraged to look to one another, nor within our-selves, for some manifestation of God. Divine truth and power were concentrated in that one unique body, in that one paradoxical life.

It is true that within the gospel narratives this logic is intriguingly unstable. At times Jesus is depicted undoing any ontological distinction between himself and others. While John identifies him as 'the true light, which enlightens everyone', Matthew describes him walking up a mountain and telling his followers: '*You* are the light of the world [*kosmou*] ... let *your light* shine before others, so that they may see your beautiful deeds [*kala erga*] and give glory to *your Father* in heaven.' Here Jesus is inviting peo-ple not merely to receive his teaching, but to participate in it by revealing goodness and truth through their own lives. He resembles Socrates, who, wrote his student Xenophon, 'in letting his own light shine, led his disciples to hope that they would attain to such excellence by imitating him.'

The 'one and many' logic, which for all its instability and ambiguity shapes these powerful, enigmatic gospel texts, was consolidated by a theological tradition insistent on Christ's metaphysical uniqueness as 'the only Son of God'.

In his *Theologico-Political Treatise*, published to great controversy in 1670, Spinoza ventured an equivocal interpretation of this doctrine. He was prepared to say that God was present in Christ as long as this meant that Christ 'perceived things truly and accurately'. And perceiving things truly and accurately meant attaining a full understanding of God and of things in relation to God. Here Spinoza undoes the distinction between revealing and perceiving – between being something, and knowing or believing it – that is intrinsic to the Christian logic of incarnation. Spinoza thought that when you fully perceive something, you become one with it, you embody it. 'In this sense,' he wrote, 'we can say that God's Wisdom, that is, a Wisdom surpassing human wisdom, assumed a human nature in Christ, and that Christ was a way to salvation [*et Christum viam salutis fuisse*].'

Henry Oldenburg, the Secretary of London's Royal Society, was disturbed by these unorthodox views. He sent Spinoza a letter asking him to 'clarify and soften the things in the *Theologico-Political Treatise* which caused trouble to your Readers'. This is what Spinoza wrote in response: 'We must think quite differently about the eternal son of God, i.e., God's eternal wisdom, which has manifested itself in all things and chiefly in the human

85

mind, and most of all in Jesus Christ.' That does indeed clarify things, though it does not soften them as Oldenburg had hoped. Spinoza was willing to acknowledge Christ's distinctiveness only in the course of insisting that this was a matter of degree, not a difference in essence or in kind. His comparative phrasing evokes a sliding scale of divine manifestation, pertaining to 'all things', but to a higher degree in human minds, and 'most of all' in Jesus's mind. While there may be differences between Christ and other human beings, there is no ontological division between them – nor between humans and any other beings.

So Spinoza refused to divide 'all things' into the one and the many: one person who manifests God, and all the rest who receive this revelation (or fail to do so). Instead, 'all things' manifest 'God's eternal wisdom'. This is, I think, simply an unfolding of his proposition, in Part I of the *Ethics*, that 'Whatever is, is in God.' Being in God, for Spinoza, means sharing or participating in God's nature, and thereby expressing or revealing it, to a certain (and variable) extent – just as each wave expresses the nature and the power of the sea.

Following Spinoza on this question is not at all a matter of denying that Jesus was (or is) God incarnate, at once human and divine. It is a matter of pluralizing this concept of incarnation. That was Lord Gifford's message to the good people of Granton when he gave his lecture on the avatars of Vishnu one chilly March night in 1880: he linked the Sanskrit *avatar* to 'the Christian word *incarnation*' and remarked that 'in all religions incarnations are known.' Speaking of incarnations in the plural makes it possible to ask of anyone not just: what does she believe, and how does she act? But also: who is she? What does her life make manifest in the world? How does her light shine?

When Goethe and the German Romantics took up Spinozism, they emphasized that human beings channel the creative power of God or Nature. Adapting Spinoza's view that some things manifest divine nature more intensively than others, they thought divinity was expressed above all by artists – exceptionally creative individuals. Weimar, home of Goethe and Schiller, became a new pilgrimage site for spiritual seekers who worshipped the miracle of Art. Travelling to the town in 1803, having been exiled from France by Napoleon, the redoubtable Madame de Staël found Goethe 'full of grace and philosophy'; even his bad moods 'passed like clouds round the foot of that mountain, on the summit of which his genius is placed'. Such divine incarnations were rare, of course – just a few great men – but it was nevertheless a radical claim that divinity was not embodied in Christ alone.

In the 1840s, while Eliot was discovering Spinoza, Kierkegaard was grappling with this inheritance. Affirming traditional Christian logic, he suggested that the question for each individual was whether they reacted with offence or faith when confronted with the paradox of Christ as divine incarnation. Yet he also wanted to know how truth becomes incarnate within each person's life – a question haplessly pursued in his queer auto-fictional novella *Repetition*. In Kierkegaard's willingness to ascribe truth to subjectivity there is an echo of Jesus's claim that he *is* the truth. A fault line between epistemic and existential truth – between perceiving or knowing truth, and living truthfully – ran through his entire authorship, and into the twentieth century's more secular existentialism, with its ideal of personal authenticity.

*

In chapter II I drew some conceptual lines, suggesting that the difference between singularity and generality mirrors the difference between biographical and philosophical enquiry – enterprises captured by two different questions: 'Who am I?' and 'What am I?'. Yet for Spinoza, the highest, intuitive kind of knowing sees singular things, rather than identifying their generic properties. Knowing something in its singularity – as a 'who' rather than a 'what' – means understanding both how it is causally related to other finite things and how it is dependent on God.

So the question 'Who am I?' is theological as well as biographical. It asks how some particular being shares in, and manifests, the divine nature. With Spinoza's help, we can distinguish a biographical knowing that traces a life as 'part of nature' – shaped by, and expressive of, its natural-cultural milieu – from a theological knowing that sees this life's being-in-God. We may do this while remaining undecided about the metaphysical relationship between these ways of knowing. Are they dual and different, or one and the same? That depends on your interpretation of Spinoza. Either way, seeing a life as at once natural and theological – at once human and divine – means receiving it as an incarnation.

Whether we read them reverently or sceptically, the gospels are tremendous exemplars of theological biography. In these life stories, the meaning of the life in question lies in its relationship to God. Since that life is an incarnation – embodied, visible, vocal, tangible and vulnerable to pain – its theological meaning is inseparable from its relationship to the world: how it is seen and received; how it sees and receives others. 'Who do you say that I am?' Jesus asks his disciples. This is not a biographical question that could be answered by recounting

a life story. It is a theological question – yet it was decisive for Jesus's life story. It shaped the extraordinary path
he carved through the world. The gospels depict a man
who understands himself in terms of this doubled significance. Of course, the gospel writers interpreted and
expressed his life in creative ways. They, too, had to draw
a line, find or make a path through their materials.

*

In her early twenties, the woman who would become
George Eliot borrowed a copy of Spinoza's *Theologico-
Political Treatise* from a doctor who, having attended
Coleridge in his last years, had been infected by the poet's
Spinozism. After reading the treatise, young Mary Ann
Evans confided to a friend that she 'considered herself a
revelation of the mind of the Deity'. Her Spinozism deep-
ened as she translated the *Ethics* in the 1850s, and then
found expression in her fiction.

Daniel Deronda, Eliot's final novel, proposes a
Spinozist vision of individual lives embodying both an
entire social milieu and a divine truth. Its fascinating
heroine, Gwendolen Harleth – charismatic, foolish,
morally flawed, vulnerable, brave, complex yet entirely coherent – is a new kind of literary character, at once
utterly singular and archetypal. Like a disco ball spinning
from a nightclub ceiling, her soul hangs in the centre of
the novel, reflecting and illuminating everything around
her. She mirrors essential features, often inward and hidden, of other characters, which in turn reflect the work's
great themes: Daniel's rootlessness and longing for his
mother – reflecting a wider Jewish experience of exile
and yearning for a motherland; the covert sadism of her
wealthy husband Grandcourt – reflecting the cruelty of

the British Empire beneath a civilized veneer; Mordecai's visionary, prophetic powers – reflecting the novel's own searching orientation to the future. As an abused wife, Gwendolen mirrors Mirah's shame at being forced to perform as a singer and actress – reflecting the experience of bodily subjugation that framed the Victorian 'Woman Question'. In her hopes for a musical career, she mirrors the artistic ambition of Daniel's mother, Alcharisi – reflecting how ruthlessness and fragility twist through the creative life.

Furthermore, Gwendolen embodies a succession of archetypes. She is kaleidoscopic; Eliot often draws our attention to her remarkable mobility. In the novel's opening scene she is the gambler, and through its early chapters she is the young witch, casting her spell on everyone around her. At an archery tournament and a fox hunt, Gwendolen is resplendent as Diana, the fierce, chaste hunter-goddess. Traversing the spectrum from virgin to whore, she eventually morphs into a weeping, penitent Mary Magdalene. She is both a needy child and a consoling mother, as in a beautiful scene near the end of the novel where she and Daniel weep together and dry one another's tears. This climactic mirror-image enacts a moment of contact between two companion souls, integrating elements that were hitherto separated. Gwendolen has been a child who clung to her mother, resisted becoming a woman; Daniel, rejected by his mother and thus prevented from being a child, perpetually cast himself in a maternal role, taking care of others. Now these two halves come together, and each person grows into the whole. Gwendolen finds her maternal power, while Daniel finally yields to the child within him. It is a scene of mutual understanding, consolation and love. It is also a scene of parting: they are saying goodbye to one another, at least for this lifetime. Typically of Eliot, this is an incarnation – of the Great Mother, perhaps – not in an autonomous individual, but in a co-dependent relationship. It reflects the Kabbalistic idea of companion souls, detailed in her *Daniel Deronda* notebook.

When Eliot translated Spinoza's *Ethics* in the 1850s, she had reached for the word 'archetype' to translate *exemplaria* – a choice probably influenced by Goethe, whose biography Eliot's new partner, George Lewes, was writing while she worked on her translation. The concept of archetype had passed from its metaphysical role in Platonic thought (including the Kabbalah) to its proto-biological status for Goethe and Schelling, on its way to the psychological, anthropomorphic usage popularized by Jung and still prevalent today. All three levels of meaning are condensed in *Daniel Deronda*, a novel that anticipates other insights of psychoanalysis, such as the link between 'suppressed experience' and symptoms of hysteria and neurosis.

As I drafted and redrafted the chapter on *Daniel Deronda* in my biography of Eliot, I kept thinking about Diana Spencer, the fairytale bride who presided over my 1980s childhood. Demure Diana showing off her sapphire ring, then crushed into a gilded carriage with her big puffy wedding dress, then waving to the crowds from the palace balcony – these scenes rose vividly to mind. Gwendolen's performance as the virgin hunter-goddess Diana seemed to me uncanny, given all the parallels between Gwendolen and Princess Diana: their double lives as ordinary women and archetypal English goddesses; their charisma, fragility, elegance and complexity; their unhappy childhoods and belief in their own specialness; the bitter disappointment and humiliation scarring their married years; the contrast between their privileged, glamorous outward lives and their secret desperation. If Eliot was not actually clairvoyant, she was remarkably prescient in understanding how all these ingredients would combine to produce the nervous symptoms, including an eating disorder, that are present in her portrait of Gwendolen as a despairing young wife.

I devoted half a paragraph at the end of my biography to this comparison. When I sat down with my editor to review the manuscript, he pursed his lips on turning to that page and said something like '*Must* we have this stuff about Diana...?' He had drawn one of his wavy lines in the margin. This distinguished publisher of history and biography, Oxford-educated and pinstripe-suited, probably thought that Princess Diana was not a serious or interesting person. Perhaps he was alarmed by a sudden suspicion that my erudition and controlled prose guarded the heart of another irrational woman. Yet Diana, like Gwendolen, exemplifies how a human life reveals the *kalon* precisely because she was no Saint Theresa or Mahatma Gandhi, but a lover of trashy novels and nice clothes who, it is rumoured – and I want to believe it – once pushed her stepmother down the stairs. While Diana, like Gwendolen, surely has her demonic side, she also shines with a beauty that is not just physical but truly moral as she touches AIDS patients, comforts sick children and strides amidst land mines. People described her as radiant or dazzling; they recognized that *kalon* quality as soon as they saw it. And she shone all the brighter through years stained by moral ugliness: Thatcherism, *American Psycho*, *The Selfish Gene*. Surely this is why even my fiercely unsentimental Mancunian grandmother wept when news broke of Diana's death; why millions of people plunged into mourning that summer; why just the other day I found myself reduced to tears by a fuzzy

YouTube video of Elton John singing 'Candle in the Wind' at Diana's funeral.

Eliot's copious notes for *Daniel Deronda* include a striking cosmological image copied from a lecture by John Tyndall, the Irish physicist and mountaineer who proved the 'greenhouse effect'. One autumn night in Liverpool in 1870, Tyndall explained that the tail of a comet is a hundred million miles long, yet its compressed matter could fit in a horse-drawn cart. 'A sky as vast as ours could', he said, 'be formed from a quantity of matter which might be held in the hollow of the hand.'

Pettiness is what we first perceive in Gwendolen. She is shallow, vain, silly, preoccupied with her 'small inferences of the way in which she could make her life pleasant'. She cuts a tiny figure in a novel swept by tides of world history – tides that are dwarfed, in turn, by a dance of planets and stars evoking both ancient gods and the marvels of modern physics. 'What in the midst of that mighty drama are girls and their blind visions?' asks *Daniel Deronda*'s narrator. 'Could there be a slenderer, more insignificant thread in human history than this consciousness of a girl...?' Yet Gwendolen's trivial life plays out a cosmic struggle between good and evil. Recall Eliot's advice to her friend Jane: 'See how diffusive your one little life may be.... One lives by faith in human goodness, the only guarantee that there can be any other sort of goodness in the universe.' Gwendolen's soul, ensnared in the bourgeois marriage plot her author has devised for her, is still, as Eliot wrote in her notebook, 'a complete citizen of the higher world & stands in immediate connection with all the Sephiroth'. The question that opens the novel – 'Was she beautiful, or not beautiful?' – asks whether it is really the *kalon* that animates Gwendolen's flashing eyes, or some demonic force. Throughout the novel she tries and fails to choose the good; the spark of *kalon* in her soul seems in danger of dying out.

In the end, Gwendolen resolves to 'be better'. (Not too much better, I hope.) She is, Eliot suggests, a 'vessel' containing 'all the wondrous combinations of the universe'. Here the metaphor for a human life shifts from a 'slender thread' to a capacious vessel. This shift mirrors the miraculous transformation accomplished by writing. Gwendolen, who exists in Eliot's imagination in multiple dimensions (symbolic as well as spatial and temporal), is rendered on the page as a line: a slender thread of ink. Yet this line conjures a vessel that contains a cosmos. Like the comet-tail squished inside a cart, Eliot has squeezed a vast world into a line, which unfolds into a world again for the reader – even a plurality of worlds.

I have said that *Daniel Deronda* looks to the future, whereas Eliot's previous novels all recalled the past with their distinctive blend of nostalgia and irony. This new orientation, together with its form and themes, make it a post-Christian work of philosophical fiction, comparable to Nietzsche's *Thus Spoke Zarathustra*, published just seven years later in 1883. By post-Christian I mean not that Christianity is disproved or rendered unbelievable, but that its cultural hold is loosened so that it becomes one world among others, and open to critique on moral, political, philosophical or spiritual grounds.

Daniel Deronda depicts a decadent Christian establishment complicit in the brutalities of Empire. It closes with a geographical reorientation, as Daniel sets sail for 'the East', leaving Gwendolen behind. Eliot's decision to leave her heroine's life unfinished was another shift from her previous literary practice. We, the readers, are likewise unfinished, somewhere in the middle of our lives. Now we are invited to stand beside Gwendolen and look with her into the future, toward a rising sun, instead of glancing back at the sunset of a life that, like Dorothea's, has completed its journey by sinking into an unvisited tomb. This modern heroine's 'happy ending' is neither a marriage nor a grave, but a search for goodness.

If we wonder what spiritual possibilities lie ahead, a clue can be found in the alternative logic of incarnation encoded in the novel's literary form, inspired by both Spinozism and the Kabbalah. If Gwendolen's apparently insignificant life expresses not just a vast cultural and psychological world – an intensely rich human milieu – but also a deep, possibly divine or cosmic goodness that impels souls to search for it, then every life might be 'read' in this way. Every life might be, as Spinoza put it, a manifestation of God. Gwendolen's ordinariness and her averagely flawed character are theologically crucial. *Even here*, Eliot seems to be telling us, there is transcendence – a stretch of the soul, a glimpse of something shining, perhaps not far away at all.

Rather than casting one man as the embodied God, and all others as witnesses and recipients of this revelation (willing or unwilling, capable or incapable), the aesthetic logic of *Daniel Deronda* entails mutual reciprocity. This logic is unfolded into an image in that final scene between Gwendolen and Daniel, where they weep and comfort one another – echoing yet transfiguring traditional images of the Madonna and Child. Each person both embodies and perceives, reveals and receives – what? What truth, what goodness, might be coming into being, if not only the God disclosed by Jesus, documented in the New Testament and worshipped by the churches built upon it? This is the question Eliot leaves us with. This is what Gwendolen is searching for – and if even *she* can search for it, so can we.

*

George Eliot's life traversed the milieu I've evoked in these last two chapters, comprising Platonism, Judaism, Spinozism, Romanticism, as well as the tangled history of Christianity – a history formed, in part, by the question of who exactly Jesus was. Her path came to an end in 1880, four years after she finished *Daniel Deronda*. During the following decade Nietzsche (who poured scorn on Eliot's work) announced the death of God and wrote his esoteric new gospel: *Thus Spoke Zarathustra*. Its hero resembles the wild, solitary Jesus who withdrew from the crowds into the mountains; Zarathustra spends most of the book living as a hermit in a mountain cave. Although this work is self-consciously post-Christian, it leaves intact – more intact, indeed, than in the gospels themselves – the incarnational logic that divides a single figure from the uncomprehending multitudes. Nietzsche's Zarathustra is a Romantic hero: an extraordinary man on the inaccessible summit of his mountain. Unlike Jesus in the synoptic gospels, he is not a character we can connect to imaginatively and emotionally. Nor does his story have much narrative or intellectual coherence. Zarathustra remains as remote from the reader as from the crowds he disdains.

For these reasons I find *Thus Spoke Zarathustra* more or less unreadable. I mention it partly to highlight Eliot's originality and literary skill; it's not easy to write a good philosophical novel, and Eliot succeeded where Nietzsche failed, and Kierkegaard too (see: *Repetition*). The comparison with Nietzsche also helps to situate her late work in its philosophical landscape: the waning years of a century transfigured by Spinozism, as well as by new scientific theories of life, evolution and society that had provoked seismic theological controversies. In this landscape, looking out towards the vacant plains of the coming century, it was possible to envisage a wider world.

Daniel Deronda's symbolic turn to the East prefigures the movement of the next generation – that of Gwendolen's children, if she has any – who begin a new chapter in the history of Spinozism. No one exemplifies this eastern turn better than Romain Rolland: writer, historian, anti-fascist campaigner. As a young philosophy student in Paris in the 1880s, Rolland experienced a life-changing 'illumination' (*éclair*) while reading Spinoza's *Ethics*. He would describe it many years later in a spiritual memoir titled *Le Voyage intérieur*:

> *Natura naturans* and *Natura naturata* are one and the same. "Everything that is, exists in God." And I too, am in God! ... Not only my body and my spirit, but my whole universe, bathe in the endless seas of *Space* and *Thought* ... in the fathomless immensity I hear ... other unknown seas, Attributes without number, inconceivable and infinite. And yet all are contained in the Ocean of Being.... Nor is it merely a matter of understanding, but the heart-beat of a co-existence.

Inspired by Spinoza's emphasis on intuition, especially by his claim that 'we feel, we experience that we are eternal', Rolland spent the next couple of years elaborating a new philosophical principle: 'I feel, therefore it is.' Rolland's 'Spinozism of sensation' rested on an experience of non-duality:

> past and future meld into one, as into an eternal present. Billions of sensations, little droplets that grow, come closer together, and disappear in order to come back again to the Ocean of Being.... It is these infinite waves of the Divine Sea whose slow palpitation I feel in my heart.

For Rolland as for many of his peers, the Great War politicized his free-spirited, Nietzschean rejection of Christianity. Those devastating years intensified his sense of Europe's moral crisis and his disillusionment with the Catholic Church. In the 1920s he turned to India's spiritual traditions. He published a biography of Gandhi, followed by biographies of Ramakrishna, a revered Bengali mystic, and Vivekananda, Ramakrishna's best-known disciple.

As he worked on these books, Rolland was corresponding with Sigmund Freud. He asked Freud to analyse *le sentiment océanique*: the Spinozist 'feeling' that Rolland believed he shared with Ramakrishna and Vivekananda. Freud wrote *Civilization and Its Discontents* in response to this request. In its opening pages Freud summarizes his exchange with Rolland and confesses that it 'caused me no small difficulty. I cannot discover this "oceanic" feeling in myself. It is not easy to deal scientifically with feelings.' The dialogue between Rolland and Freud, and the ideas it generated on both sides, would shape debates about psychology, mystical experience and comparative religion through the twentieth century. At the heart of those debates are questions about the unfolding path of a human life – about the ideals, practices and relationships that enable a life to grow and flourish, and about continuities and differences across diverse cosmological milieux.

Rolland prefaced his *Life of Ramakrishna* with a statement of his own Spinozist principles:

Ramakrishna lies very near to my heart because I see in him a man and not an "Incarnation" as he appears to his disciples. In accordance with the Vedantists I do not need to enclose God within the bounds of a privileged man in order to admit that the Divine dwells within the soul and that the

soul dwells in everything – that Atman is Brahman: for that
... is a form of nationalism of spirit and I cannot accept it.
I see God in all that exists. I see Him as completely in the
least fragment as in the whole Cosmos.... The very greatest
of men is only a clearer reflection of the Sun which gleams
in each drop of dew. That is why I can never make that
sacred gulf so pleasing to the devout, between the heroes
of the soul and the thousands of their obscure companions
past and present.

While the convergence of Spinozism and Hinduism
in Rolland's writing reflected that particular cultural moment, it had a history stretching back to the
seventeenth century. Pierre Bayle, one of Spinoza's earliest critics, saw in the *Ethics* a pantheistic doctrine 'very
current in the East Indies' and 'almost universal' among
'Hindu Pandits [*Pendets indous*]'. For Bayle this was not
a good thing, but many of the Romantics who embraced
Spinozism were drawn to Indian thought. Coleridge
described Spinoza as 'the sternest and most consistent of
the Adwitamists', 'Advaita' being the non-dualist strand
of Hindu philosophy. Particularly influential was Herder,
a prolific philosopher and poet whose appreciation of
Spinoza in *God: Some Conversations* (1787) – proposing
that 'for him the idea of God is the first and last, yes, I
might even say the only idea of all' – was soon followed
by *Thoughts on Some Brahmins* (1792). Herder's devotional
response to Indian art, religion and philosophy shaped
the mythical image of India in German Romanticism, just
as his reading of the *Ethics* reshaped Spinoza's image from
dangerous atheist to God-intoxicated sage.

This Romantic legacy shows up in Lord Gifford's
pursuit of 'felt knowledge', which led to him to research
Brahman and Vishnu as well as Spinoza's concept

of substance, and in the new academic discipline of 'Indology' that was emerging at that time. In 1894 the German Indologist Max Müller – who had delivered a cross-cultural series of Gifford Lectures in Glasgow the previous year – argued that 'Brahman, as conceived in the Upanishads and defined by Śankara, is clearly the same as Spinoza's *Substantia*.'

There's a chance the link between Indian philosophy and Spinozism goes right back to Spinoza himself. The most extensive seventeenth-century western work on Hinduism was written by a Dutch missionary, Abraham Rogerius, and published in Leiden in 1651. At that time Spinoza was eighteen or nineteen: a scholarly young man, passionately interested in philosophy and theology, with every reason to be curious about a new book on Indian traditions. Rogerius had spent about a decade on the Coromandel coast of south-east India (now Tamil Nadu) and devoted much of his stay to learning about the local customs and religion from a group of Brahmins. His book, *De Open-Deure tot het Verborgen Heydendom* (The Open Door to Hidden Paganism) was soon translated into French and German, and became an important source for Herder.

I love the idea of Spinoza sitting up by candlelight studying Rogerius's book, learning about the ten avatars of Vishnu and south India's five principal Śiva shrines – including Arunachala, the mountain of light. Then he finds at the back of the book a prose translation of two Sanskrit lyrics attributed to the fifth-century philosopher Bhartrihari: this is the first transmission of an Indian text in any European language. Its author recommends renouncing worldly things and retreating to a mountain cave; he emphasizes the transience of this life and contrasts ordinary human ignorance with the enlightened knowledge and beatitude of the yogi or sage, who attains total contentment resting in eternal and impersonal divine being. Could this text have prompted Spinoza's experiments in renunciation, recounted in his earliest work, the unfinished *Treatise on the Emendation of the Intellect*? Did it make him think differently about God and incarnations? The evidence is scarce, but it is thrilling to imagine these ideas flowing into Spinoza's life, all the way from the Coromandel coast, and all the way to the end of the *Ethics*.[*]

---

[*] 'For the ignorant man – besides that he is agitated in many ways by external causes, and possesses no true satisfaction of mind, lives without true consciousness of himself, of God, and of things, and as soon as he ceases to suffer, ceases also to exist; while, on the other hand, the wise man, so far as he is such, has a soul scarcely moved by external things; he has true consciousness of himself, and of God, and of things in virtue of an eternal necessity; he never ceases to exist; and always possesses true repose of mind. If the way which I have shown to lead to this result appears very difficult, it can nevertheless be found' (*Ethics* 5, prop. 42, scholium; translation by George Eliot).

V. ARUNACHALA

In 1896 a sixteen-year-old boy left his home in south-east India and travelled two hundred miles to Tiruvannamalai, where there is a sacred mountain named Arunachala. First he lived in the basement of the huge temple to Śiva that lies at the foot of the mountain. Later he moved into a cave in the mountain itself. He lived there for sixteen years, then moved to another place just up the hill. He gained a reputation as a great spiritual teacher, Ramana Maharshi – 'Ramana' from his given name, Venkataraman, and 'Maha rishi' meaning 'great seer'. A small community of devotees gathered near his cave. His mother tracked him down, and in 1914 she joined his community. When she died she was buried beside Arunachala. Ramana walked down the hill daily to visit her shrine. One day he stayed there, taking up residence in the thatched hut that had been built over his mother's tomb. Over the next few years an ashram gradually took shape around him: a dining room, a few huts for devotees, a cowshed and a small meditation hall where Ramana slept and received visitors. He lived in the ashram until his death in 1950. During the fifty-four years since he'd arrived in Tiruvannamalai, he had not travelled more than a mile from Arunachala.

Why did young Ramana leave home, without telling his family where he was going, taking only enough money for his train ticket? There are two ways of answering this question. Most accounts emphasize a 'transformative experience' – though Ramana himself did not put it this way – that had occurred a few weeks beforehand: the kind of thing William James would soon be analysing as a 'mystical state of consciousness' in his Gifford Lectures on *The Varieties of Religious Experience*. It began with an intense fear of death. This wasn't the first time he had contemplated what it means to die. Four years earlier, when his father passed away, he had tried to figure out what exactly it was that had lived and then died – who had existed and then ceased to be? Now, though, it was different: not just a sequence of thoughts, but a spontaneous awakening.

Years later he described it to his devotees.

> This body is going to die, I said to myself ... and I came to the conclusion that when it was dead and rigid ... *I* was not dead. I was conscious of being alive, in existence. So the question arose in me, What is this "I"? Is it the body? Who called himself the "I"? ... I felt that there was a force or current, a centre of energy playing on the body, continuing regardless of the body's rigidity or activity, though existing in connection with it.

Sixteen-year-old Ramana did not have a vocabulary adequate to this so-called 'experience'. He thought it might be *avesam*, a Tamil word meaning possession by a spirit. 'The fact is, I did nothing. Some higher power took hold of me and I was entirely in its hand.'

He didn't discuss this with anyone, but his daily life changed. He became indifferent to his schoolwork. He spent his time 'absorbed in contemplation' of the inward force or flow that remained continually present to him. During those last weeks at his family home, he recalled, he 'was only feeling that everything was being done by the current and not by me'. This current drew him to the local temple in Madurai almost every evening. 'I would go and stand there for a long time alone before Śiva, Nataraja [a form of Śiva as cosmic dancer], Meenakshi [Śiva's consort, to whom the Madurai temple is dedicated] and the sixty-three saints. I would sob and shed tears.' Here he 'trembled' with an emotion that was neither joy nor sadness.

Soon after he arrived at the Arunachala temple, Ramana encountered sacred texts from the Advaita tradition of Vedānta, a philosophical monism prominent in south-Indian Śaivism. Monism is the view that all reality is essentially one; the Sanskrit word *a-dvaita* means 'not two' or 'non-dual'. Advaita Vedānta affirms the identity of all things with Brahman or Śivam, the impersonal divine Self (*Atman*) that sustains the universe. In Vedānta, reality has three essential properties: it is eternal and unchanging, and it shines with its own light (*svayam prakāśa*). The Self is real in this sense. It is pure, radiant consciousness without distinction between knower and known, subject and object. Until we see Self as our true nature, the delusion of being a separate, small self causes a lot of suffering. These teachings fitted with the new understanding that arose during Ramana's contemplation of death.

That dawning insight has often been described as 'Self-realization', and Ramana's own teachings have been situated in the Advaita Vedānta tradition. Yet before he left home he had never heard of Brahman, let alone read the scriptures and commentaries that expounded Advaita doctrines. The only religious texts he knew were some Tamil poetry, the *Periyapuranam* (a twelfth-century epic poem telling the life stories of sixty-three Tamil saints devoted to Śiva), and the Psalms he studied at his Christian missionary high school.

Counterposed to the story that begins with a 'transformative experience' is Ramana's own account, which attributes his 'Self-realization' to Arunachala. On this account, his experience was a symptom or side-effect, rather than a cause; it was not, therefore, 'transformative'.

This distinction matters because it concerns the very structure of spiritual practice: if specific experiences are thought to bring about change, they become a goal that shapes the practice. We shall see that Ramana repeatedly dispelled this kind of view, just as he challenged the very concept of Self-realization. Realization implies attainment, whereas for Ramana everything was due to grace. And Arunachala's grace had merely unfolded a truth that had always been there, uncovered the nature he already was. To speak of either 'realization' or 'experience' implies that *something is happening to someone* – a construction belonging to the dualistic way of thinking that Ramana transcended.

As a young child Ramana had imagined Arunachala as a heavenly realm: 'the holiest place, the holiest state, God himself.' He was amazed to learn from a relative, who had recently been there, that it was actually a real mountain, just a few hours by train from Madurai.

Arunachala is in fact a long-established pilgrimage site. Its temple, dating back to at least the seventh century, houses one of south India's five principal Śiva lingams. These lingams correspond to the five elements recognized in Indian cosmology: earth, air, fire, water and space. A lingam is an embodiment of Śiva, usually formed of stone. The inner shrine at Arunachalesvara Temple houses the fire lingam; the mountain itself is also considered to be a fire lingam. 'Arunachala' means 'dawn mountain', dawn (*arun*) being the fiery hour of sunrise. Here Śiva is said to have manifested as an infinite column of light. Every winter, on the full moon in the month of Kartika, a beacon is lit at the summit of Arunachala. Millions of pilgrims flock to the site at this time, and the fire can be seen for miles around.

In 1896 Ramana was following in the footsteps of

numerous Tamil seekers and saints who had travelled to Arunachala over the centuries. Some of them took up residence in the mountain's caves – the closest a person could come to Śiva himself. Ramana left a note for his family, telling them not to look for him. He wrote that he was leaving 'in search of my father and in obedience to his command'. This commanding 'father' was Arunachala. Instead of signing his name, Ramana simply drew a line.

Achala means 'motionless' as well as 'mountain'. If some object – the sun, for example – is reflected in a lake, the reflection is *chala*: wavering, shimmering, while the object itself is *achala*, unwavering. A mountain is quintessentially *achala*. Inside Ramana's cave – inside the mountain – the stillness of Arunachala is profound.

When Ramana was asked about this mountain's special sanctity, he explained that while the other lingam temples are the abodes of Śiva, Arunachala *is* Śiva. This distinction is linked to Śiva's unique stillness at Arunachala. Its fire is the fire of *jnana* (wisdom; true knowledge), which 'burns the ego to destruction'. The whole mountain, Ramana explained to one of his devotees, 'is pure *jnana* in the form of a hill. It is out of compassion for those who seek him that Śiva has chosen to reveal himself in the form of a hill visible to the eye. The seeker will obtain guidance and solace by staying close to this hill.'

Like other Śaiva sages who went there before him, Ramana composed hymns to Arunachala. His first, written around 1914, describes the seeking soul as a bride and Lord Arunachala as its bridegroom, though it also addresses Arunachala as 'father' and 'mother'. Here Ramana wrote that the mountain instructs through silence. More devotional hymns and poems followed, all written in the first and second person. Many of them blend autobiography with theology. In 'Necklace of Nine

Gems', Ramana describes a double birth, to his biological parents and to Arunachala:

> In Tiruchuzhi, the holy town of Bhuminatha,
> I was born to Sundara and his good wife Sundari.

> As mother and father both, you gave me birth and
>   tended me...
> You came to abide in my mind, you drew me to
>   yourself, O Arunachala.

Another hymn, 'Eight Stanzas to Arunachala' (*Aruna-chala Ashtakam*), invokes the mountain while recalling Ramana's childhood:

> Look, there it stands as if insentient.
> Mysterious is the way it works, beyond all human
>   understanding.
> From my unthinking childhood,
> The immensity of Arunachala had shone in my
>   awareness.
> But even when I learned from someone that it was
>   only Tiruvannamalai,
> I did not realize its meaning.
> When it stilled my mind and drew me to itself and
>   I came near,
> I saw that it was stillness absolute.

The mountain transcends religious differences: 'In order to reveal Yourself at last as Being and Awareness, You dwell in different forms in all religions'; 'Like the string that holds together the jewels in a necklace, You penetrate and bind all beings and the various religions.' Having begun in 'unthinking childhood', the poem concludes with images of returning to a source – a blissful 'ocean home':

> The raindrops showered down by the clouds, risen
> from the sea
> Cannot rest until they reach, despite all hindrance,
> once again their ocean home.
> The embodied soul from You proceeding may
> through various ways self-chosen wander aimless
> for a while,
> But cannot rest till it rejoins You, the source.
> A bird may hover here and there and cannot in mid-
> heaven stay.
> It must come back the way it went to find at last
> on earth alone its resting place.
> Even so the soul must turn to You, Arunachala,
> and merge again in You alone, Ocean of bliss.

The love for Arunachala expressed in these hymns shaped Ramana's life. He lived in or on the hill for over twenty years. After he moved down to the ashram he took daily walks, morning and evening, along the mountain's lower slopes. His one political act was to write a legal deposition opposing the Indian government's plan to seize control of Arunachala and fell its trees; he cited sacred texts, oral traditions and his own poetry as evidence.

Considered in the light of Arunachala, the 'Self-realization' experience so prominent in most biographies of Ramana looks less like a decisive event than the final death rattle of a self that had long being drawn and subdued by the mountain. Perhaps numerous lifetimes had journeyed to this moment of union and dissolution.

*

People who came to the ashram were struck by Ramana's humility and his simple life. He owned a loincloth, a dhoti (or sarong), a water pot and a walking stick. He refused to let anyone treat him as a special person, and shared in the communal work of cooking, cleaning and building. He did not present or publicize himself as a teacher – which was remarkable in a religious culture where initiation from a guru is usually considered essential. However, he was willing to answer questions. Apart from his hymns to Arunachala, most of his published teachings take the form of Q&A dialogues documented by devotees or visitors, and in some cases revised and edited by Ramana himself.

His responses to questions reveal the difficulty of conveying his wisdom (*jnana*) in words, since its core quality was stillness, silence, simple being. He repeatedly explained that so-called Self-realization 'is not attaining something new or reaching some goal that is far away, but simply being that which you always are and always have been.... It is false to speak of realization. What is there to realize?' Asked by someone whether they should renounce householder life and retreat to the forest, or stay at home, he replied: 'You are to remain in your true state.'

Ramana encouraged his questioners to ask themselves, 'Who am I?' We might hear this as a biographical question, concerning the subject of actions and experiences. But Ramana was not seeking to elicit a life story. Still less was he after a definition or theory of selfhood. Over time, 'Who am I?' would draw the questioner into inward contemplation, shifting attention from thoughts to the thinker, from perceptions to the perceiver. With practice, Ramana advised, the individual feeling of 'I' would eventually dissolve into its source and vanish, leaving only the divine Self.

While Ramana became renowned for this method of self-enquiry, his most important teaching was his own silence, in which he communicated his awakened presence to those who came to sit with him. Many visitors described an experience of deep stillness and peace, different from anything they had felt before. Some called this grace, since all they had to do was receive it. Once they came to Ramana, the intellectual questions they had planned to ask often dropped away. As thoughts subsided, a simple faith or knowing would arise in their place. When one student asked him why he didn't go out and preach Advaita, Ramana replied, 'How do you know I am not doing it? ... Preaching is simply communication of knowledge. It may be done in silence too.'

Whether through his communicative silences or through his directions for self-enquiry, Ramana sought to connect people with their true nature. Dispelling any duality of self and other, guru and disciple, he enveloped them within his *jnana* so they could share it, as he himself had been drawn into the stillness of Arunachala.

*

I first saw a photo of Ramana around 2007, on a mantelpiece in a terraced house in Sale, a south Manchester suburb, where for several years – most of my thirties – I attended a weekly meditation group. At the heart of this group was our elderly teacher, Russel Williams. This ordinary-looking man, outwardly indistinguishable from a thousand other beige-clad pensioners, had undergone a spiritual awakening decades earlier, not long after the war. For some time he could neither understand nor explain it. One day, lonely and bewildered, he cried out for help, and suddenly a profoundly peaceful presence was with him.

When he asked where this came from, Ramana's face – which he had never seen before – appeared to him. Years later Russel saw a photograph of Ramana and recognized the face from his vision. He felt connected to Ramana and taught in a similar way, often in silence.

I might well have dismissed Russel's inexplicable vision, had I not repeatedly experienced for myself the silence and stillness – that Arunachala quality – that he was able to share with us. How was this possible? On those evenings in Sale I often thought of Spinoza, teaching his little group of students that they were all modes of substance, conscious and embodied, and interconnected, porous, so that the boundaries between modes can be transcended, one finite being flowing into another. Spending time with Russel at once quieted our minds and expanded our intellectual horizons. In his company, over the years, my cosmological milieu gradually changed. I found myself inhabiting a much wider agnostic sphere, stretched by new possibilities.

This personal vignette contains an ambiguity similar to Ramana's own story. The mysterious transmission from Ramana to Russel in the 1940s echoes the transmission from Arunachala to Ramana in the 1890s – and I somehow find myself transported to a possible world where such things happen. Yet alongside or within that astonishing world is another, more familiar world of labs, libraries and lecture halls, where explanations can be sought and theories offered.

That photo of Ramana on a Manchester mantelpiece was just one token of his diffuse influence, carried from India to the West. This began around 1930, when Paul Brunton, a young journalist from an East End Jewish family, set off for India 'in search of the Yogis and their hermetic knowledge'. Brunton had moved in London's

113

esoteric circles during the 1920s, attending theosophical meetings and helping to establish an occult bookstore, the Atlantis Bookshop, still going strong in Bloomsbury. The theosophists believed that ancient India possessed the highest wisdom – and that modern Europeans were best placed to recover it.

Brunton chronicled his travels in *A Search in Secret India*, published in 1934. It begins with Brunton confessing that India brought about a 'vital change' in his thinking. Though not converted to 'any Eastern creed', he arrived at 'a new acceptance of the Divine'.

> As a child of this modern generation, which relies on hard facts and cold reason, and lacks enthusiasm for things religious, I regard [this] as quite an achievement. [My] faith was restored in the only way a sceptic could have it restored, not by argument, but by the witness of an overwhelming experience.

An 'unassuming hermit' – this turns out to be Ramana – was responsible for his change of heart. Brunton described his visits to many teachers in India and presented his encounters with Ramana as the culmination of his quest. The book ends with our sceptical author leaving the ashram, looking up at Arunachala, wondering at the 'strange spell' it has cast over him. Finally he says goodbye to 'the Maharishee':

> He has strangely conquered me and it deeply affects my feelings to leave him. He has grappled me to his own soul with unseen hooks which are harder than steel, although he has sought only to restore a man to himself, to set him free and not to enslave him. He has taken me into the benign presence of my spiritual self and helped me, dull Westerner

that I am, to translate a meaningless term into a living and blissful experience.

If Ramana changed Brunton's life, Brunton also changed his – a fact that raises complicated questions about the ethics of life writing as well as the dynamics of agency and appropriation in a colonial milieu. *A Search in Secret India* was an instant bestseller. Many readers were inspired to travel to Tiruvannamalai to see this amazing Maharishi for themselves. From then on, there were no more quiet days at the ashram.

In 1936 Somerset Maugham travelled to India, eager not 'to shoot a tiger or to sell anything ... nor to see the Taj Mahal', but to 'meet scholars, writers and artists, religious teachers and devotees'. One afternoon he visited the busy Ramanashram. Maugham used this experience in his 1944 novel *The Razor's Edge*; he took its title from the Katha Upanishad, a founding text of Vedānta praised by Emerson and Schopenhauer. Set in the 1920s and presented as a true story, the novel is about a young American, traumatized by the war, who is transformed by his visit to a fictionalized Ramana, renamed Sri Ganesha. In the hands of Maugham – a bohemian writer from a family of prosperous lawyers – a young westerner's encounter with Ramana became a story about dropping out of high society, varying the theme of *The Moon and Sixpence*, whose stockbroker-turned-artist hero was modelled on Paul Gauguin. *The Razor's Edge* sold over three million copies and was almost immediately made into a Hollywood film, released in 1946. As a teenager I was gripped by this book after stumbling across it in my local library, though I had no idea it was drawn from life; then I found and loved Maugham's autobiographical novel *Of Human Bondage*, not yet knowing that its title came

115

from the fourth book of Spinoza's *Ethics*. In those days I liked nothing more than to lie in bed and dissolve into whatever book I was reading, and I've finally recovered this habit – the trick is to find the right books: the ones you simply want to read, where your desire, your love flows unimpeded through the pages, and maybe where the author once dissolved in them too.

Maugham returned to the subject of India at the end of his career, after Ramana had died, in an essay titled 'The Saint'. Here he described his visit to Ramana's ashram and expounded some elements of Hinduism: the Upanishads, Brahman, meditation, reincarnation. He mentioned the *Vivekacudamani*, an Advaita text ascribed to the eighth-century Śaiva philosopher Śankara, whose 'supreme achievement', wrote Maugham,

> was to take the speculations of the Upanishads and in conjunction with them construct the religious philosophy known as Advaita. It is an absolute monism, or, as Indian scholars prefer to call it, a non-dualism. Its main principles are Brahman and Reincarnation. Brahman is the only reality. The world is a manifestation of Brahman.

Two thirds of 'The Saint', however, is devoted to Ramana's life story. Before he visited the ashram Maugham had, he tells us, read the autobiography of Saint Theresa and the lives of Francis of Assisi, Catherine of Siena and Ignatius Loyola – 'But it never occurred to me that I might be so fortunate as to meet a saint in the flesh.' True to the tradition of hagiography, his 'Life' of Ramana ends with the saint's exemplary death.

> At sunset he asked to be raised to a sitting position, the ritual posture of meditation. A group of his disciples began

to chant the hymn to Arunachala which long ago he had
composed. His eyes opened and tears of ecstasy rolled down
his cheeks. His heart stopped beating. The Maharshi had
entered the Reality of the One. At the moment he died, a
comet moved slowly across the sky, reached the top of the
sacred hill, Arunachala, and disappeared behind it. It was
seen by vast numbers, and they ascribed the strange phenomenon to the passing of a great soul.

This was one of many iterations of Ramana's story that
appeared in the West, both during and after his lifetime.
Memoirs by his Indian devotees were translated into
English, the language of Empire. As with Brunton and
Maugham, Ramana's life story became interwoven with
the stories of seekers and disciples who encountered
him and wrote about him. There is the poignant story
of Heinrich Zimmer, a pioneering scholar of Indian art
and literature, who was influenced by Jung and col-
laborated closely with Joseph Campbell. Zimmer was
intensely interested in Ramana. He longed to go to India
to see him, but was thwarted first by financial setbacks,
then by Germany's Nazi government (his wife was half
Jewish), and finally by the outbreak of the Second World
War. After Jung visited India in 1938, the first question
Zimmer asked him was whether he had been to see
Ramana. To Zimmer's amazement, he had not, despite
– or perhaps because of – Ramana's renown as a master
of Self-realization, an ideal Jung also advocated. The last
work Zimmer completed before his untimely death in
1943 was a German translation of Ramana's teachings,
introduced with an crudite biographical essay (and a
somewhat ambivalent preface by Jung). Here Zimmer
compared this 'holy man' of Arunachala to the Buddha
and to Jesus Christ. Ramana's simple replies to questions,

wrote Zimmer, transmitted 'India's ancient message': 'a message telling us to transcend the "I", to renounce the illusion of the world, to become a saviour full of redeeming knowledge.'

In the 1950s, not long after Ramana died, Arthur Osborne published the first English collection of his teachings. Osborne had dropped out of Oxford and joined a Sufi group before winding up at the ashram in 1945, fresh from a prisoner-of-war camp. His wife and three young children had gone there ahead of him. In his autobiography *The Mountain Path, My Quest*, Osborne recounts how his daughter Kitty was the first to meet Ramana – or 'Bhagavan', as his devotees still call him:

> She stepped into the hall where he used to sit, a small, beautiful child with curly gold hair, bearing a tray of fruit in her hands, the customary offering. Bhagavan pointed to the low table beside his couch where such offerings were placed, and she, misunderstanding, sat down on it herself, holding the tray in her lap. There was a burst of laughter. "She has given herself as an offering to Bhagavan," someone said.
> A day or two later my wife entered the hall and sat down. Immediately Bhagavan turned his luminous eyes on her in a gaze so concentrated that there was a vibration she could actually hear. She returned the gaze, losing all sense of time, the mind stilled, feeling like a bird caught by a snake, yet glad to be caught ... She wrote to me that all her doubts had vanished; her objections no longer mattered ... The most beautiful face, she told me, looked commonplace beside him, even though his features were not good. His eyes had the innocence of a small child, together with unfathomable wisdom and immense love. For her this was the time of grace and wonder ... She felt his power and guidance constantly.

*

Why did Ramana's life story seize so many western imaginations? Perhaps Arunachala's mysterious power drew these European seekers, just as it had drawn Ramana in his youth. But Arunachala and its saints had been there for centuries. What happened in the last century to make Ramana's story take root and flourish in the West?

The answer to this question involves a broad and complex narrative about the entanglements of colonialism and post-Christian spirituality. Many Spinozists, Romantics and Transcendentalists – Coleridge, Emerson, Whitman – had been drawn to Vedānta, preceded by Herder at the end of the eighteenth century, if not by Spinoza himself.

Prophetic post-Christian visions such as *Daniel Deronda* and *Thus Spoke Zarathustra* were followed by more visible shifts in the religious landscape, spurred by theosophy, a movement as influential as it was controversial. Carl Jung, born in 1875, as Eliot was finishing *Daniel Deronda*, was a prominent representative of the next generation. Jung loved Nietzsche and especially *Zarathustra*, and like Nietzsche he was the rebellious son of a Protestant clergyman. By 1910 he was telling Freud, his mentor, that 'religion can be replaced only by religion ... 2000 years of Christianity can only be replaced by something equivalent.' He saw that this 'something equivalent' had to include myths, stories and images – narratives that would 'evoke ... that age-old animal power which drives the migrating bird across the sea.' In 1932, as Paul Brunton left the ashram, Jung concluded that 'every one' of his European patients

fell ill because he has lost what the living religions of every age have given to their followers, and none of them has

119

really been healed who did not regain his religious outlook. This of course has nothing to do with a particular creed or membership of a church.

In retrospect, the World's Parliament of Religions, held in Chicago in 1893 to coincide with the spectacular Columbian Exposition (marking 400 years since Columbus 'discovered' the Americas), appears as an inaugural event in this new milieu. Though staged by progressive Protestants, the Parliament of Religions was a post-Christian moment insofar as Christianity was here on display as one religion among many. The organizers, convinced of the superiority of their religion, were keen to perform their enlightened 'tolerance' of 'non-Christian faiths'; more conservative Americans warned they were 'coquetting with false religions' and 'planning treason against Christ'. The Archbishop of Canterbury refused to attend. Perhaps these critics were right to be wary: Japanese delegates rebuked missionary Christianity for 'devastating' and 'trampling' their nation 'under the disguise of religion', while Vivekananda, the charismatic star of India's delegation, announced that Hinduism had 'taught the world ... universal acceptance.' Local and national newspapers reported his striking claim that 'The Hindu refuses to call you sinners. Ye are the Children of God, the sharers of immortal bliss, holy and perfect beings.' Vivekananda turned the Orientalist narrative contrasting a pure, spiritual East with a materialist, political West to India's own political purposes – and all this prepared fertile ground for Ramana's story.

Paul Brunton's *A Search in Secret India* reproduced tensions that were simmering in Chicago forty years earlier. Assuming a western readership convinced of their superiority to Indians, Brunton reinforced this racist complacency even as he challenged it. Hindus were, he alleged, uncritical, incapable of distinguishing fact from fiction – yet he also felt that his own culture's 'cold reason' proved a hindrance to the spiritual wisdom he sought in the East. His journey inverted the missionary project: here was a literate Englishman submitting to the teachings of a 'jungle sage' and spreading them through Christian (or post-Christian) society. Still, Brunton's attitude remained condescending, and his eventual reverence for his 'Maharishee' seems as miraculous as Ramana's powers of transmission.

Ramana's emphasis on experience helps to explain his appeal to westerners. This was hardly an innovation: the medieval *Vivekacudamani*, which Ramana is said to have translated from Sanskrit into Tamil, taught that the eternal Self (*Atman*) is 'the common experience of all'. And it was more than a hundred years since the Romantics, above all Schleiermacher, had primed Europeans to see religion as a matter of 'feeling'. Romain Rolland's 'Spinozism of sensation', with its oceanic feelings, carried this Romantic tradition into the twentieth century, bringing a new focus on Indian exemplars. As Rolland's own example shows, Ramana's experiential teaching now spoke to westerners for whom other sources of knowledge and meaning – cold reason, hard science, church dogma, blind faith or some murky blend of tradition and convention – were increasingly discredited. Experience was replacing belief as the cornerstone of religious life, as William James's Gifford Lectures made clear. In his concluding lecture James quoted Vivekananda's summary of Advaita Vedānta:

> Why does man go out to look for a God? ... It is your own heart beating, and you did not know, you were mistaking

it for something external. He, nearest of the near, my own self, the reality of my own life, my body and my soul – I am Thee and Thou art Me. That is your own nature. Assert it, manifest it.

Like James's lectures and Vivekananda's modernized Vedānta, Ramana's life story offered a spiritual path accessible to all. Its core appeared to be a transcultural, ahistorical experience – an idea that was, ironically, very much of its time – rather than esoteric teachings encoded in foreign texts or requiring initiation into a guru lineage. The narratives popularized by Brunton and Maugham do not mention that Ramana valued scriptures and literary, scholarly work – that he translated the *Vivekacudamani*, for example, or that his imagination was shaped by the *Periyapuram* before his 'Self-realization' occurred. They downplay his deeply devotional outlook, rooted in Tamil Śaiva *bhakti* traditions. Framed like this, Ramana's awakening at the age of sixteen, knowing nothing of Brahman or of Śankara, proved that spiritual success required only the willingness to 'dive within' and question yourself. His inclusive teachings attracted westerners who were drawn to perennial philosophies or inter-faith practice, or lured by an exotic 'alternative' to their own culture.

This life also manifested a powerful sense of destiny, both alien and attractive to westerners. In a new century oppressed by the burden of choice – whether James's 'will to believe'; the existentialists' ideal of heroic decision; the Nietzschean mantra of self-creation, value-creation; or simply the perplexing question of which spiritual path to follow in a pluralist world – Ramana's submission to his destiny could be consoling, even liberating.

Ramana did not choose to go to Arunachala: he was pulled by the mountain. When his mother found him in

1898 and begged him to come home, Ramana, who was unable to speak at that time, wrote her this note: 'The divine ordainer controls the fate of souls in accordance with their past deeds. Whatever is destined not to happen will not happen – try how hard you may. Whatever is destined to happen will happen, do what you may to stop it.'

The aspect of his own fate he found hardest to accept was his fame, especially after Brunton's book came out: the crowds that streamed to the ashram, their endless questions, the quarrels among his devotees. This was not the life he'd expected when he took refuge in Arunachala. He enjoyed working in the ashram – he chopped vegetables, fed the cows, sewed leaf plates, supervised building projects – but receiving visitors in the meditation hall each day was more a duty than a pleasure. Occasionally he talked about leaving the ashram. Yet he stayed; in any case, the crowds would follow him up the mountain if he retreated to a cave. While he always steadfastly refused to sign his name, ever since writing his farewell note at sixteen – causing endless problems at the Post Office – he accepted the inconveniences of being 'Sri Ramana Maharshi' as part of the destiny ordained by Arunachala.

When Ramana was asked why he did not engage in India's struggle for independence, he responded that Gandhi had likewise surrendered to the divine. 'He must do what he has come for. We must do what we have come for,' Ramana told his students. There are striking parallels as well as striking differences between these two remarkable lives. Gandhi was born ten years before Ramana, in 1869, and died two years before him. He was an ardent Rama devotee and is said to have chanted the Ram mantra all his life, including with his final breaths when he was shot in 1948. He was influenced by Advaita Vedānta – which he first encountered via theosophists in

London around 1890 – and came to espouse a universal notion of religion that 'transcends Hinduism' and seeks union with 'the truth within'. Both Gandhi and Ramana taught by example, a method that Gandhi regarded as essentially non-violent. Ramana's disciple Papaji, who spent a period as Gandhi's attendant before becoming a renowned spiritual teacher himself, perceived in both men an exceptional radiance. Gandhi, he recalled,

> had the most sattvic body I have ever seen. It was copper-coloured and on a subtle level it was glowing with the light of Brahman. The only body I have seen that was as beautiful as his was the Maharshi's. Both of their bodies used to shine.

Sattva means purity, harmony, goodness and peace – rather as the Greek *kalon* encompasses beauty, fineness and nobility. Papaji's memory of glowing bodies is a fitting symbol of *sattva*'s diffuse effects. It also illustrates the ethic of exemplarity practiced by both Ramana and Gandhi: they were quite literally shining examples for their followers.

While Ramana's surrender took him to Arunachala, Gandhi's surrender empowered his political vocation. The disjunction between these two lives illustrates the distinction between the concept of a self and the concept of a life. Even if the self dissolves, or never existed in the first place, the life remains vivid, its story compelling. For Ramana and Gandhi, self-surrender to the divine found expression in two highly distinctive paths, dramatically visible in the world. If Ramana's individual self was dissolved in the ocean of Brahman as a salt doll is dissolved in the sea – a traditional Advaita metaphor – the life that came to be named Ramana Maharshi had sharp, shining contours. It was filled with specificities: a Śiva temple, a mountain path, a mother, a father, sixty-three Tamil saints; an ambitious English theosophist, a little girl with curly blonde hair, a restless novelist. It was a singular expression of a milieu combining ancient traditions, in which hills are divine and cows are sacred, with India's complex relations to a colonial power in flux and in crisis. Ramana's life story interlaced with other equally singular life stories – of his mother, of his Indian disciples, of western seekers, dropouts, tourists and scholars.

Retelling this story now, I would love to know how it is that Brahman manifests as Arunachala – how an ocean creates a wave; how Spinoza's finite modes 'flow from eternity'; how infinite Self takes shape as a single life. How does eternal being yield an existence so definite, so singular, that arises and passes away? How does what is formless coalesce into so much beauty? Perhaps these questions would dissolve in the deep silence of Arunachala, just as that salt doll dissolves in the sea. Meanwhile, the questions feel bittersweet. Of course they do: they arise from the longing, the perplexity and the poetry of our condition as finite modes, somewhere in the middle of our lives.

As I researched Ramana's life story I read more and more about the milieu that shaped it: memoirs of life in the ashram, and scholarly studies of Hinduism, Advaita Vedānta, Tamil Śaivism, and Indology itself. I tightened my grasp of grand, sprawling concepts: Romanticism, Orientalism, colonialism, exoticism, hermeneutics, anthropology's 'ontological turn'. I chased critique, even a few critiques of critique. I quickly learned to reflect earnestly on my own position in all this. I saw myself in Zimmer, the scholar; in Brunton, the seeker-tourist caught somewhere between devotion and exploitation; and in Maugham, the urbane writer – all of them Romantics, in

125

their way. At every turn, my fear of naivety, my dread of being a cliché, alerted me to a blind will to cleverness that runs through academic life, shaping our egos and forming our disciplines.

None of this strenuous thinking illuminated Ramana's surrender to the grace of Arunachala. His own understanding of his life seemed incommensurable with the historical and critical narratives I'd accumulated. And what he taught – *how* he taught – was fundamentally different from everything I'd learned in the academy. Eventually I suspected that however much I read, whichever theory I reached for, this disjunction would remain. Twenty-five years had passed and I was back where I'd started: with Kierkegaard, who reached a similar conclusion in the 1840s about the sum total of cutting-edge empirical and conceptual knowledge on the one hand – back then academics were excited about biblical criticism, rationalist theology, Hegelian dialectics – and the truth of Christianity on the other. Kierkegaard saw how absurd it would be to build a theory to bridge the gap between theory and this incommensurable truth. Indeed – and what a cruel twist for a brilliant young man – intellectual work might take him further away from the truth of life, the truth of God. So instead of theorizing the impasse, he ironized it. His works dramatize his contradictions: a philosopher without faith in philosophy; a scholar denouncing scholarship; an author relinquishing authority. Kierkegaard's solution, if we can call it that, was literary, performative and indirect. Same here. The best I can do, if I write, is try to write truthfully.

VI. TRANSCENDENCE FOR BEGINNERS

For an author it is especially interesting to see how other authors choose to end their books. Some pages back we considered the ending of *Middlemarch*, which summons its heroine's elusive life-as-a-whole. Kierkegaard ended *Fear and Trembling* by talking about beginnings. He cited Heraclitus, who stands right at the beginning of the history of western philosophy. Subsequent thinkers built on Heraclitus's teachings – but 'no generation learns what is truly human from a previous generation'. When it comes to matters of the spirit, and matters of the heart, 'every generation begins primitively'. For example, no generation learns to love from another. I'm not so sure about that: most of us do learn to love from our parents. But this is pretty much all we know. Otherwise we are just starting out, childishly full of love, trying to figure out how to put one foot in front of the other. Learning to love was easy; learning to lose what you love is very hard. As is learning to sit still. It helps, I've found, to consider yourself a beginner.

When I wrote Kierkegaard's life I wanted readers to encounter him as he lived, facing an uncertain future and struggling to understand himself. Instead of playing the part of an omniscient biographer, I tried to efface myself. But right at the end of the book there is a photo of Kierkegaard's much-visited grave in Copenhagen, and I am in the frame. The last paragraph describes how it felt to accompany my subject through his turbulent years, as we drew closer to his death; how it felt to encounter 'the mysterious weight of a human life, glimpsed in its entirety'.

In this book I've returned to that glimpse of one whole life – which came to me only as I finished my first

127

biography – and tried to understand it better. A whole life, elusive yet expressive, is utterly singular. It is the centre of a milieu that never entirely coincides with another life's world, and is never entirely separate from it either.

We might imagine God as containing and transcending all these worlds: the ultimate milieu, in which everything lives and moves and has its being. At the same time, some image or incarnation of God can appear within a world, maybe stiffened and cracked with time, maybe painted fresh or new-born. As Heinrich Zimmer wrote in his essay on Ramana Maharshi, such manifestations of the divine are 'supra-worldly and intra-worldly at the same time'. They are at once transcendent and immanent. Not surprisingly, this is theologically confusing, just as it is psychologically confusing that your mother is both your milieu – the world in which you first lived and moved and had your being – and a finite, fallible person in her own world, in some ways still child-like herself.

I am learning to live with these confusions. Helped by the pantheon of exemplars that have shaped my milieu – people I've known personally and writers I've read closely – I have asked if the concept of incarnation can be applied to every life. Looking at a life this way prompts us to wonder what truth – and what mystery – it embodies and transmits.

But what about the life-writer? While she is contemplating and (re)constructing another person's life, her own life is unfolding, partly through her biographical work. What does that work – a strange mixture of philosophy, art and fact-finding – embody and reveal? Of course, this question cannot be answered in the abstract. Nor should it become a merely personal question. Let me tell you one more story.

Over the last year or so, as I worked on the lectures that

became this book, I got to know the painter Celia Paul. She was born in 1959 in south India, where her father was a missionary priest, and moved to England with her family when she was five. She now lives and works in an attic flat in central London – just around the corner from the Atlantis Bookshop. Early in her career she decided that she wanted to paint people she loved. She painted many portraits of her sisters, her husband, her son, most of all her mother. These paintings, quiet yet full of feeling, document Paul's search for the truth of a human life – and they find beauty in this search, even when it involves loneliness, sadness and loss. 'When you work from life,' she told me, 'the subject is there like a measuring stick of the truth.' Talking to Celia and looking at her paintings helped to clarify my own questions about what it could mean for a philosopher to work from life.

Paul has written an autobiography titled *Self-Portrait* and a book about the artist Gwen John that blends biography and memoir. Reading each other's books, we found we'd been pursuing similar paths of thought and feeling through life writing. These paths converged as we began to write to one another. 'I am sure there can't be just one incarnation. The whole of nature disproves it,' Celia replied, when I told her I was drawn to the Spinozist and Hindu view that many beings, maybe all beings, can be incarnations or manifestations of God. The elemental images that came to mind as I drafted my Gifford Lectures – the mountain, the path, the sea – had already recurred in Paul's paintings. Among my favourites are *My Mother and the Mountain* (1994–2020), and a soft-ground etching titled *My Mother and the Sea* (1999). Last summer she prepared to go to Venice to work on a new portrait of Proust, her favourite writer, while I started re-reading *In Search of Lost Time*. We were both thinking about interdependence

129

and grief. We discussed the difficult choice between close attachments and the solitude that sometimes feels necessary for intellectual and creative work.

We had also wrestled with similar questions about how much we should allow ourselves to appear alongside our subjects. As portraitist or biographer you are always there: making choices, asking questions, drawing lines. Is it better – more truthful – to show your hand and eye at work, or to efface yourself as much as possible? A philosopher, of course, might ask herself the same question.

When you work from life, in art or in philosophy, life's relentlessly relational texture becomes palpable. Your relationship to your subject is woven into the truth you're trying to uncover and convey. Because Paul painted those closest to her, the relationships rendered in her paintings are intimate and profound. Every Tuesday and Friday her widowed mother used to get up very early and take the train from Cambridge to come and sit for her in the morning light. She would walk down to Bloomsbury from King's Cross, slowly climb the eighty stairs to Celia's flat, and turn up at 8 a.m. dishevelled and out of breath. She obediently sat still for hours. In the afternoon, Celia would watch her leave:

> My heart ached as I said goodbye and watched her rounded back as she made her way slowly down the stairs, gripping the bannisters nervously as she went. I would look out of the window and watch her as she walked away from my flat, a hesitant but determined little figure among all the crowds of tourists outside the British Museum. I could still see her as she walked down Great Russell Street, until she reached the street that led into Russell Square, and then I would lose sight of her.

This mother gave herself to her daughter's art because she understood how much it mattered to her. When I suggested that Celia's repeated portraits returned this devotion, in a different form, she agreed. 'My mother was never properly seen in her daily life,' she wrote to me. 'She found the attention I gave her healing in some way. She didn't mind what I made of her, she just needed to be looked at.' Celia's portraits of her mother distil the beauty of those hours in which two human beings gave one another time.

In 2015, a few months after her mother died, Paul began a large painting of her four sisters in mourning. That year she also made studies of the sea, a waterfall, a stream before and after heavy rain. 'After my mother died, everything seemed in flux,' she wrote in her memoir.

> All that had been structured and consoling before had broken up and dissolved. The only meaningful subject appeared to me to be water. I felt that time itself was like water, a powerful current that had dragged my mother away and that was also pulling me in the same direction. There was some comfort for me in this thought.

She kept thinking she had painted her last seascape, then a new one would come along, as if carried on another wave of grief. These sea paintings share the intimate, devotional quality of Paul's portraits: artist and subject giving one another time.

As an eighteen-year-old student at the Slade, Paul felt alienated by the life-drawing classes. 'It seemed so artificial to me to draw a person one didn't know or have any involvement with.... I needed to work from someone who mattered to me. The person who mattered most to me was my mother.' As I read these words I felt a little surge

of happiness. Also a pang of recognition: as a philosophy student I had suppressed similar thoughts. Nothing mattered more than my mother's life and her recent death; no questions were more pressing than who she was, or had been, and what it was like for her to die. And who would I be, now that the world we'd shared had ended? I learned that these thoughts had nothing to do with philosophy, and imagined I would one day grow out of them. Paul, meanwhile, had defied her teachers – or at least she did not simply try to please them. She allowed herself to think about what (and who) really mattered to her, made this a defining principle of her practice, and stayed true to it for decades. Over those years she created beautiful works of art, filled with wisdom.

Paul's repeated portraits of her mother were, she explained, 'necessary because I loved her. Their necessity gave them their force.' Her stubborn, child-like preference for those she loves, and has a chance of knowing intimately, eschews any pretence of detached objectivity. For me – still obsessed with George Eliot – this resonated with the passage in *Middlemarch* where the narrator admits that because he or she is concentrating on a few people in a small town, there is no time to examine 'the universe'. The irony of this remark lies in the principles of exemplarity and incarnation that govern Eliot's late novels – principles at once aesthetic, ethical and metaphysical. These works disclose the inner lives of people who would otherwise be obscure, make them matter intensely to us, and then insist: *here* is truth, here is goodness, here we glimpse something at once singular and universal, comic and cosmic.

Commenting on the art of biography, André Maurois argued that 'objectivity and detachment are the supreme aesthetic virtues'. A biography should, he added, be

133

truthful rather than flattering. Yet compassion and even love are not the same as flattery. Celia Paul's paintings, like Eliot's novels, exhibit a partiality that stretches to devotion and reverence, and prove that this is entirely compatible with truthfulness. These artists' acutely partial interests determine where and how they direct their attention – yet the attention itself is clear-eyed, neither idealizing nor romanticizing. It looks compassionately, not sentimentally: it seems to see things as they are in order to accept them as they are. Under such a gaze, lives can become radiant.

*

Is Eliot's love for her characters, or Paul's love for her sitters, different in kind from the love proper to philosophy? A philosopher, by definition, loves wisdom itself. To pursue wisdom without interest in any extrinsic reward or recognition it might bring: this is a high ideal indeed. I repeatedly fall short of it, and I suspect most other so-called philosophers fall short of it as well. Yet we – I mean all of us – incline towards this ideal. If the very thought of it causes our hearts to lift and our minds to clear and brighten, these slight movements are signs that a real love for wisdom flickers in our souls. It is a special sort of love only insofar as wisdom is assumed to lie beyond embodied life and experience, and if the path to wisdom must lead away from attachment to finite, living, particular beings.

When we attend to the lives of philosophers, we see how their work is moved and sustained by devotion. Devotion is a repeated movement of return that expresses love. And when we ask, as a philosopher must, what is love?, the answer surely lies in this concept of devotion:

at once an action, a feeling, a relationship and an affirmation of value. Devoted partners return home to one another each night; a devoted daughter calls her elderly mother every day. A devout Catholic goes frequently to Mass; a devout Hindu goes frequently to the temple. These examples come readily to mind, but there is also the devotion of a sports fan, a gardener or a biographer. Devotion means giving yourself willingly to what you love. This is a lived love, never simply an inward feeling. Essentially active and expressive, it is a virtue as well as an affect. Devotion gives ethical shape and emotional colour to our expressive, exhibitive way of being in the world.

The word comes from the Latin verb *devovere*, meaning to vow, to offer, to dedicate, to consecrate. This little family of meanings implies freedom. Yet the devotee's freedom is tethered to her sense of the *kalon*: she feels this is something she *must* attend to. Remember how Hannah Arendt explained that the *kalon* is 'what is beautiful, as opposed to what is necessary or useful'. But something can be necessary without being useful, and the *kalon* has its own kind of necessity. In 1844 Kierkegaard argued that 'to need God is a human being's highest perfection', and a similar claim might be made about the need for beauty, which is neither logically nor causally necessary, yet spiritually necessary. This is a passionate necessity: 'a necessity that we feel, that we undergo', to borrow a phrase from Etienne Souriau's lecture on the 'Work to be Made'. It has the force of a vocation, a calling. It is moved to express itself again and again. The peculiar experience of necessity belonging to the *kalon*, felt and expressed in devotion, helps to distinguish it from other repetitive behaviours such as addiction, obsession or mere routine – despite the zones of ambiguity and transition that lie between these different modes of repetition.

Devotion may frequently lapse in distraction, doubt or fatigue. Yet devotees are sooner or later drawn back to what they love. The Latin word *religio*, a binding, evokes this idea of being tethered or re-tethered. The steadfastness of an ordinary devout life is neither *chala*, wavering and shimmering like a reflection in water, nor *achala*, the stillness of a mountain or a sun. It is rhythmic, emotional, more like the moon or the tides. It waxes and wanes, ebbs and flows, yet keeps returning. Ramana Maharshi's extraordinary devotion to Arunachala is an exception that illuminates this rule. Ramana did not keep returning to his Śivam-mountain, but simply stayed there, immersed in its stillness.

Although we philosophers often remind one another that 'philosophy' literally means 'love of wisdom', devotion is rarely invoked as a philosophical virtue. Perhaps it seems anti-intellectual, akin to the childish faith and feminine submission disdained by Enlightenment thinkers, who sought to free philosophy from the constraints of dogmatic religion. Right now – under the aspect of eternity – Spinoza is probably frowning on me waxing lyrical about devotion. He defined love as the affect of joy coupled with an idea (which might be true or false) of the cause of that joy; then he defined devotion as a love that involves wonder and linked it to imagination as opposed to true understanding. In the *Theologico-Political Treatise* Spinoza argues that religious devotion is intellectually regressive: people resist naturalistic explanations for miracles because they would rather cling to their wonder than enlarge their knowledge. In the *Ethics* he is more interested in interpersonal devotion. You feel wonder, Spinoza explains there, when you're struck by the singularity of another person – some special quality they seem to exhibit. But this shine rubs off over time; wonder fades and devotion gives way either to disillusionment and disdain, or to simple affection.

That was Spinoza's view. It is true of course that habit and custom can dull your sensibility, subdue your excitement. And yet wonder can pierce the most quotidian moments. Surely it's not just me who is sometimes struck by the singular beauty of familiar things: the tall trees on Hackney Downs, the faces of my husband and my son across the kitchen table, or the moon gracing our suburban sky.

Ever since the days of Plato and Aristotle, it has been said that philosophy begins with wonder – and perhaps it is our recurring wonder, shining through the everyday, that makes us begin again and again. When Plato used the verb *theorein* to describe how philosophers contemplate the Forms, he invoked pilgrims (*theoroi*) who journeyed to sacred sanctuaries, temples and festivals to see manifestations of divine presence. The ancient Greeks called this devotional practice *theoria*. Philosophical devotion is an active constancy that binds the fluctuating passion of thought – ignited by wonder even if it tries to push beyond it – into a regular practice of attention.

Spinoza's own life story proves this point. His tenacious search for goodness and truth is described at the start of his unfinished *Treatise on the Emendation of the Intellect*. Here he sets out a conversion narrative, in which he 'devotes' himself to 'the true good'. Spinoza finds this pursuit difficult, yet necessary. It requires him to live differently. He isn't just after a theory of ultimate reality: he wants to know eternity first-hand and share it with others. He wants his life to be an incarnation of truth and a path to beatitude.

The phrase translated here as 'devote' is *dare operam*, a common Latin idiom meaning 'pay attention'. *Dare* means to give or to offer, and *opera* means labour, exertion, effort or work. The labour Spinoza is describing is an offering of consciousness, thoughtfulness, and of course time. His philosophical way of life seemed to generate its own repetitions; it inspired devotion and work in other people. A small group of friends and students gathered around him, wanted to spend time with him, offered financial support (which he refused) and laboured in risky circumstances to publish the *Ethics* in the months after he died. Through that book, which embodies and transmits Spinoza's dedication to philosophy, he continues to inspire devotion among many readers, myself included.

Spinoza might be reassured to hear that devotion need not entail an overtly reverential attitude. While devotion may be full of feeling, its essence is the simple yet profound human act of registering the value of something by giving it attention, energy and time: the basic resources of a life. Quite simply, a life gives itself, because it loves.

I began my Gifford Lectures by recalling a younger Clare who was moved and puzzled when she encountered something she called nobility. What did that even mean? Now I have an answer for her. Nobility amounts to a capacity for love, coupled with a certain kind of bravery: the strength a vulnerable, fallible being has to muster day by day to express that love in the world. This virtue is more like *to kalon* than *to agathon* because it is not conditional – good for someone or something in particular – but simply, in itself, beautiful and fine, as will be evident to anyone with eyes to see it. Kant, as devout as he was rational, held onto this thought as he honed intricate arguments for a human goodness that 'like a jewel, shines by itself'.

138

*

I wrote the first draft of my final lecture during a trip to Skye last summer. On afternoon walks, as landscape kept shifting to seascape, philosophical thoughts blurred with my own life story in ways I felt I should resist. Up there the sea seems to me at once knowing and unfathomable: harbouring secrets, bearing witness to loss, and at times almost unbearably beautiful – all the more so as I get older. My thoughts, stretching across this sea, were rendered as helpless as my limbs and lungs and heart would be, if I swam out too far. I thought about Celia Paul painting another sea, feeling drawn by the same currents that had pulled her mother away.

I had with me *Time Regained*, the last volume of *In Search of Lost Time*. Here Proust reveals that the entire novel has been the doubled story of an artistic vocation and of a life (and its milieu) resurrected through memory. The irony of re-reading *Time Regained*, on Skye of all places, made me smile. Perhaps certain scenes would take me back to the bedroom or beach or café where I had first read them in my twenties – maybe the pages, like the hours they had filled, would smell of patchouli or sun cream or cigarettes – just as Proust's middle-aged narrator is transported to a series of past selves in past worlds, as their sensations recur: the chink of a spoon on a plate, a starched napkin against his lips, uneven paving stones beneath his feet, the taste of a madeleine dipped in limeflower tea. This didn't happen to me; perhaps it never happened to Proust either.

Inspired by Ruskin and George Eliot, Proust wanted to fuse art and philosophy in the medium of life writing. 'Can I call this book a novel?' he wondered as he completed an early version of it: 'It is something less, perhaps, and yet much more, recounting the very essence of my life, with nothing extraneous added, as it could be felt flowing by.' Then he crossed out those last seven words, and wrote instead 'as it unfolded through long periods of unhappiness'. Drawing on Greek and Indian doctrines of reincarnation, Proust searched for a literary form that could explore the 'great mystery of extinction and resurrection', immanent as well as transcendent to a single lifetime. He created a narrative 'encompassing many deaths and many unrecognisable rebirths'.

In his last two hundred pages Proust describes a single afternoon, when his narrator goes to a party at an old friend's house. This turns out to be a momentous day, a 'wonderful day', on which 'the aim of my life and perhaps that of art were illuminated'. As the novel ends he has a sudden intuition of a whole human life. His body, he realizes, contains all the time he has lived – 'so many memories, so many joys and desires'. After death this Time will leave his body (as if Time were his soul). Now he understands that 'all this span of time ... was my life, that it was myself ... that it bore me up, that I was poised on its dizzy summit, that I could not move without taking it with me.' Marvelling at his own enormous dimensions, he feels 'giddy at seeing so many years below and in me as though I were leagues high'.

A human body does not look very large: like a book, the space it occupies is dwarfed by the time it carries. In truth it is, concludes Proust's narrator,

as though men were perched upon living stilts which keep
on growing, reaching the height of church-towers, until
walking becomes difficult and dangerous and, at last,
they fall. I was terrified that my own were already so high
beneath me and I did not think I was strong enough to retain

for long a past that went back so far and that I bore within me so painfully. If, at least, time enough were allotted to me to accomplish my work

– he means the novel that he (or Proust himself) intends to write, and that the reader is now, finally, finishing –

I would not fail to mark it with the seal of Time ... and I would therein describe men, if need be, as monsters occupying a place in Time infinitely more important than the restricted one reserved for them in space, a place, on the contrary, prolonged immeasurably since, simultaneously touching widely separated years and the distant periods they have lived through – between which so many days have ranged themselves – they stand like giants immersed in Time.

While the semi-fictional or real lives woven through his novel are made of time, not space, Proust has reached for figurative images to describe them. They are giants, monsters; they walk on stilts as high as churches, or balance on mountaintops. Pure time, the stuff of life, is transmitted not through the book's images but through its form. The hours spent reading the novel – scattered pools of time stretched over weeks, months, possibly years – mirror the life-time Proust has recollected and reimagined from pools of memory scattered over decades. His narrator is indeed made of time: the time we have spent with him. The flow of time becomes the medium of a shared life. We have occupied his life, and he has occupied ours.

Now that he knows what his work of art will be, he begins to conceive the creative labour that awaits him. He has to devote himself to this book:

to bear it as a load, to accept it as the object of his life, to build it like a church, to follow it like a regime, to overcome it like an obstacle, to win it like a friendship, to nourish it like a child, to create it like a world, mindful of those mysteries which probably only have their explanation in other worlds, the presentiment of which moves us most in life and in art.

An extraordinary memoir of doubled devotion – her own and Proust's – was kept by Céleste Albaret, who joyfully served him night and day as his housekeeper during the years he worked on *In Search of Lost Time*.

Proust's narrator fears he has frittered away too many years; by 'lost time' he means not just time past, but time wasted. When Proust read *Middlemarch* he was fascinated by its portrait of Edward Casaubon, 'who had devoted his entire life to an insignificant and absurd study' – a terrifying prospect that must have haunted Proust's nightly labours, and also a mirror-image of the tragic romantic error, dramatized in both *Middlemarch* and *In Search of Lost Time*, of devoting your life to the wrong person. When his narrator finally begins to write, he does so in fear and trembling, not knowing whether he would finish his book, nor whether it would become

a church where the faithful would gradually learn truth and discover the harmony of a great unified plan, or whether it would remain, like a Druid monument on the heights of a desert island, unknown forever. But I had made up my mind to consecrate to it the power that was ebbing away.

*

A biography may not be a whole life's work, but the biographer must devote some portion of her own life to the whole life that constitutes her subject. She kneels before this 'giant immersed in time', traces the contours of feet the size of a childhood, reaches up for the hem of its garment, and listens for its vast heart beating. All this devout attention is mixed with the moral lapses and ambiguities that mark most intimate relationships: it is entirely appropriate for biographers to feel uneasy about using their subject's fame or talent to further their own literary careers; about exposing this frail life to public scrutiny and judgement. Such self-doubt, just like biographical devotion, is rooted in some deep, perhaps inchoate recognition of the value of a life.

Since devotion is not merely a feeling, but essentially active and expressive, it has a shining, transmissive quality. It is beautiful, this self-consecration of a life. Proust, a connoisseur of beauty, chose to end his novel with this thought – 'I made up my mind to consecrate to it the power that was ebbing away' – while suggesting that it also began with this thought. I suppose I, like many others, am drawn to the story of Ramana Maharshi because it exhibits so clearly this radiant and radiating devotion. Ramana in Arunachala is at the heart of the story, like a sun at the centre of a cosmos. Other lives circle around him. But he is not quite an unmoved mover. Especially poignant – because it is so human – is the movement of his mother's life, searching out her son, following him up the mountain, and his reciprocal movement, coming down the mountain to her shrine.

Of course we find devotional rhythms everywhere, on very different temporal and geographical scales. Over centuries, billions of people around the world have repeated Jesus's prayers and teachings, reread his life

143

story, and recalled his bodily presence. All those efforts to stay close to him echo his own extraordinary devotion to (and union with) his God. Over decades, millions of pilgrims have travelled to Ramana's ashram, and walked up and down his mountain path. During a similar period, hundreds of philosophers, theologians and historians – and their audiences – gave hours of their life to reaffirm Adam Gifford's dedication to pursuing 'the true and felt knowledge (not mere nominal knowledge) of the relations of man and the universe to God, and of the true foundations of all ethics and morals.' Handfuls of people return week after week to Christine's yoga class, and to the house in south Manchester where Russel taught meditation before he passed away. Almost every year since 1995 I've driven up to Skye and spent a week in the place where my mother used to watch the sea. Each weekday I get up early, make my son's breakfast and help him pack his bag for school.

I'm not convinced the scale matters much. It seems to me that all this is neither time lost nor time regained, but time given, and time shared.

Time lost or given; time wasted or consecrated: inscribed within all these concepts – loss, waste, gift, consecration – is an intuition about the value of a life. Proust believed that his own time would prove to have been unwasted, or redeemed, only if it were consecrated to making great art. As his biographer Jean-Yves Tadié puts it, 'he lived in order to write', and his own life – including his friendships – became a 'laboratory' to be used to that end, with all the ruthlessness this use implies. We need not share Proust's attitude to art and life to take up, and make meaningful for ourselves, his distinction between waste and consecration. While these notions seem quite different, they both imply value. When you say that something has gone to waste, you recognize a value that has been squandered. Waste has a tragic aspect, because you both imagine how things could be otherwise, and see that it's now too late to take that alternative path. Other kinds of loss may simply feel inevitable.

As a biographer examines a whole life, she will be struck by two truths: loss and return. Each person lives those truths differently, of course. We come closer to discerning their life's shape when we attend to what they lost, and what they kept returning to.

Devotional returning expresses love – and not always a happy love. Kierkegaard, for instance, gave himself daily to his literary work in a way that sometimes made him feel that God required him to suffer like Christ on the cross. He poured his time, energy and money into his writing compulsively, ambivalently, restlessly, often tortuously. To the end of her life George Eliot struggled with self-doubt and with a fierce ambition that she (and others) considered unseemly in a Christian woman, though it was part of her love and inseparable from her creative power.

Loss, like return, is intrinsically connected to love. I mean that this connection is deeper than the sad fact that, as we grow up, we realize that whatever we love will sooner or later pass away. Grasping the syllogism that everything is finite, including, therefore, things we love, is not quite the same as seeing that love belongs to the very concept of loss. Whilst all things must pass, we speak of losing – as of wasting – only when what passes is something we value, something we cling to.

Kierkegaard was criticizing his Christian culture's distorted priorities when he lamented that the loss of your self – by which he meant each human being's immense inward dimensions – 'can occur very quietly in the world, as if it were nothing at all.... Any other loss – an arm, a leg, five dollars, a wife, etc. – is bound to be noticed.' Failing to notice that your true self has been lost means failing to value it properly. Kierkegaard made a similar point about waste: 'There is so much talk about wasting a life, but only that person's life was wasted who went on living so deceived by life's joys or its sorrows that he never became decisively and eternally conscious as spirit.' Yet for Kierkegaard, this eternal consciousness is no flight from joy or sorrow. Faith, he wrote, is 'simultaneously to be out on 70,000 fathoms of water and yet be joyful'. If that strikes you as an even more challenging ideal than pure-hearted pursuit of wisdom – to swim happily in the deep cold waves, knowing they must inevitably overpower your body and carry it away – then Kierkegaard agreed with you. Such faith, he argued, is more difficult than philosophy.

Devotion and loss are two sides of the proverbial coin. They both express love. They are so deeply part of human experience that it is difficult to imagine a life lived without them. Some will say they are a characteristically human response to an indifferent universe: expressions of our struggle to generate meaning and value, or of our unfortunate propensity to mire ourselves in personal attachments that make us suffer. Value, they will say, is something we confer upon the world – not some intrinsic or objective feature we discern in things. But these interpretations seem less compelling when we consider ourselves part of 'God or Nature'. Then the experiences of devotion and of loss, in which we reveal ourselves to be – like my Mancunian grandmother – at once fierce and tender-hearted, may be read as a sign that love flows through us because it is an element of reality itself: like water, like air, like fire.

Loss and return are brought together in mourning. This is not the same thing as grief – the sadness, anger and sheer pain of loss – though of course mourning and grieving can coincide. Having lived so long in mourning, I have come to think that this is the path devotion carves in the absence of its object. We are such expressive beings that our losses inflict the further suffering of feeling that our love suddenly has nowhere to go, nothing or no one to offer itself to. Mourning allows us to go on. This is a devotional movement: a movement of return that attends to what is lost, perhaps wasted; bears witness to its value and recalls its singular qualities.

Perhaps each new moment calls us to mourn our lost time, but of course we find special ways to mourn a whole life that has ended. We build shrines, plant trees, say prayers, gather flowers, swap stories, frame photographs, light candles, burn incense, allow tears to flow and dry and flow again. Surely it is no coincidence that our acts of mourning, like our acts of friendship, are so conspicuously offerings of time – ephemeral things bestowed, child-like, on eternity.

Writing a life or painting a portrait only exhibits the gift of time, as precious as it is commonplace, that we offer one another every day. These gifts are a communion of souls. Since we are the living giants described by Proust, tottering on our stilts of memory and time and growing taller still as each hour passes, we're still touched by other giants – entire lives, largely mysterious, which gave birth to us and walked here before us, forging the paths we follow.

Endnotes

20 *'He spoke freely of what he thought, and most often his thoughts were of God …':* Stanley Jaki, *Lord Gifford and His Lectures* (Edinburgh: Scottish Academic Press, 1986), pp. 93–4. This account was written in 1891 by John and Mary, Lord Gifford's brother and sister.

20 *'a part of the Infinite, for the Infinite cannot be infinite if it does not include everything':* See Jaki, *Lord Gifford and His Lectures*, p. 98.

20 *'Hinduism or Brahmanism … is a monism, a monotheism and a pantheism …':* Adam Gifford, 'The Ten Avatars of Vishnu' (Granton, March 1880) in Jaki, *Lord Gifford and His Lectures*, p. 128.

21 *a very thoughtful talk to the local Philosophical Society on 'Attention as an Instrument of Self Culture':* 'In a very important sense, attention is the only faculty which is directly, purely and entirely at our command and at our choice … Let attention only be yours, attention awakened by pure desires and stimulated by noble emotions, attention intense and keen, dwelling upon elevating objects and ideas, reiterated upon the good, and the beautiful and the true, till these and these alone are loved and honoured; let such attention be daily and hourly practised' – Adam Gifford, 'Attention as an Instrument of Self Culture' (Greenock, November 1874) in Jaki, *Lord Gifford and His Lectures*, p. 108.

21 *'any religion or way of thinking':* From Lord Gifford's Will, reproduced in Jaki, *Lord Gifford and His Lectures*, pp. 73–4.

21 *'the true and felt knowledge (not mere nominal knowledge) of the relations of man and the universe to God …'; 'this knowledge, when really felt and acted upon, is the means of our highest well-being':* From Lord Gifford's Will, reproduced in Stanley Jaki, *Lord Gifford and His Lectures*, p. 73 (italics mine).

23 *flowing, sharing (or participating) and expressing:* See Spinoza, *Ethics* I, P17, scholium; Spinoza, Letter 12 in *The Collected Works of Spinoza*, ed. Edwin Curley (Princeton, NJ: Princeton University Press, 1985), vol. 1, p. 203; Clare Carlisle, *Spinoza's Religion: A New Reading of the Ethics* (Princeton, NJ: Princeton University Press, 2021), pp. 92–111; Gilles Deleuze, *Expressionism in Philosophy: Spinoza*, trans. Martin Joughin (New York, NY: Zone Books, 1990).

23 *'pure immanence':* See Gilles Deleuze, *Spinoza: Practical Philosophy*, trans. Robert Hurley (San Francisco, CA: City Lights Books, 1988), pp. 29, 88; also Etienne Balibar, *Spinoza: From Individuality to*

...   *Transindividuality* (Rijnsburg: Eburon, 1997), which repeats Deleuze's claim that Spinoza's substance does not transcend individuals, yet develops an alternative notion of transcendence, which Balibar calls 'transindividuality'.

23   *Spinoza's Neoplatonic tendencies*: In Spinoza's *Short Treatise on God, Man and His Well-Being*, God's causal power is described as 'emanative': see *The Collected Works of Spinoza* vol. 1, p. 80. One 'Spinozist' passage in Plato is *Timaeus* 49d–50a, which characterizes particular things as (like Spinoza's modes) not really things at all, but qualities lacking any stability, while 'that *in which* each of these things appears' is (like Spinoza's substance) a stable entity.

23   *the variety of possible meanings of transcendence*: As Bruno Latour argued, transcendence can be synonymous with immanence: see *An Inquiry into the Modes of Existence*, trans. Catherine Porter (Cambridge, MA: Harvard University Press, 2013), p. 299. A similar point has been made by Vedānta scholars – see T. R. V. Murti's preface to Rama Kanta Tripathi's *Spinoza in the Light of Vedānta* (Varanasi: Bhargava Bhushan Press, 1957) – and by classical scholars and theologians who defend non-dualist interpretations of Platonic participation: see Eric Perl, 'The Presence of the Paradigm: Immanence and Transcendence in Plato's Theory of Forms', *Review of Metaphysics*, vol. 53 (1999), pp. 339–62; David C. Schindler, 'What's the Difference? On the Metaphysics of Participation in a Christian Context', *Saint Anselm Journal*, vol. 3, no. 1 (2005), pp. 1–27; Cornelio Fabro and B. M. Bonansea, 'The Intensive Hermeneutics of Thomistic Philosophy: The Notion of Participation', *Review of Metaphysics*, vol. 27, no. 3 (1974), pp. 449–91.

24   *'whatever we desire or do, or cause to be done, in virtue of our ... knowing God'*: Spinoza, *Ethics* IV, P37; on religion, see the first scholium to this proposition. For Spinoza, 'religion' is not a matter of doctrinal belief or institutional belonging, but a virtue – see Carlisle, *Spinoza's Religion*, pp. 164–83.

25   *'We feel, we experience that we are eternal'*: Spinoza, *Ethics* V, P23, scholium.

25   *Spinoza argued that error consists in a lack of knowledge; more specifically, in mistaking a part for the whole*: See Spinoza, *Ethics* II, P17, scholium and P35.

29   *an uncivilized, morally pure person from some other place or time who lives in simple harmony with nature*: This idea stretches back at least to Montaigne, but postcolonial scholars have traced its most pernicious

... construction to the mid-nineteenth century. Charles Dickens published an essay titled 'The Noble Savage' in his journal *Household Words* in 1853, and John Crawfurd, a Scottish physician, historian and colonial administrator who ended his life as President of the Ethnological Society of London, promoted the concept in 1859. See Ter Ellingson, *The Myth of the Noble Savage* (Berkeley, CA: University of California Press, 2001) and Tabish Khair, 'Dickens and the Noble Savage', *Dickens Quarterly*, vol. 39, no. 3 (2022), pp. 269–75.

29   *'shining in brightness'*: Plato, *Phaedrus*, 250b–d.

29   *'what is beautiful as opposed to what is necessary and useful'*: Hannah Arendt, *The Life of the Mind*, ed. Mary McCarthy (New York, NY: Harcourt, 1978), p. 20.

29   *'I can will* to kalon *but I cannot do it'*: Romans 7:18.

29   *the* kalon *simply is noble or beautiful or fine, to anyone with eyes to see it*: This account of the *kalon* drew on Gabriel Lear, 'Plato on Learning to Love Beauty' in *The Blackwell Guide to Plato's Republic*, ed. Gerasimos Santas (Oxford: Blackwell, 2006), pp. 104–24 and 'Response to Kosman', *Classical Philology*, vol. 105, no. 4 (2010), pp. 357–62; Rachel Barney, 'Notes on Plato on the *Kalon* and the Good', *Classical Philology*, vol. 105, no. 4 (2010), pp. 363–77; Jonathan Lear, *Imagining the End: Mourning and Ethical Life* (Cambridge, MA: Harvard University Press), pp. 15–19.

30   *'enigmatic good'; 'unmarked concept'*: Lear, *Imagining the End*, p. 16; Barney, 'Notes on Plato on the Kalon and the Good', p. 369.

30   *the difficult and elusive path to beatitude is summarized as* omnia praeclara: Spinoza, *Ethics* V, P42, scholium.

30   *She chose as her exemplars a 'hero'*: See Linda Zagzebski, *Exemplarist Moral Theory* (Oxford: Oxford University Press, 2017). The book was published before Vanier was found to have sexually abused numerous women who were under his spiritual guidance at the L'Arche community he founded.

31   *'precisely because of his reality that there is much about Mr McMahon that I do not know ...'*: Lear, *Imagining the End*, p. 52.

35   *Socrates used this exercise to change his students' souls*: Martha Nussbaum, *Love's Knowledge: Essays on Philosophy and Literature* (Oxford: Oxford University Press, 1990), p. 16. See Jonathan Lear, 'Allegory and Myth

... in Plato's Republic' in *The Blackwell Guide to Plato's Republic* (Oxford: Blackwell, 2006), pp. 25–43.

37 *'requires a complete life'*: Aristotle, *Nicomachean Ethics*, second edition, trans. Terence Irwin (Indianapolis, IN: Hackett, 1999), 1098a, 1100a, pp. 9, 12; *Eudemian Ethics*, trans. Brad Inwood and Raphael Woolf (Cambridge: Cambridge University Press, 2013), 1219a-b, pp. 16–17.

38 *'traces of everything that happens in the universe, even though God alone could recognise them all'*: G. W. Leibniz, 'Discourse on Metaphysics', §8 in *Discourse on Metaphysics and Other Essays*, trans. Daniel Garber and Roger Ariew (Indianapolis, IN: Hackett, 1991), p. 8. For Leibniz this is true of all individual things, not just of human persons or lives. But perhaps the elusiveness is especially salient in the case of a human life (our own or someone else's), precisely because we care so much about knowing it. As Leibniz wrote to Antoine Arnauld in 1686, 'the concept of *myself in particular* and of every other individual substance is infinitely more extensive and more difficult of comprehension than a specific concept like that of the sphere ... Certainly, since God can form and in fact does form this complete concept which contains what is sufficient to account for all the phenomena which occur to me, this concept is possible, and it is the genuine complete concept of what I call myself' – *The Leibniz-Arnauld Correspondence*, trans. H. T. Mason (Manchester: Manchester University Press, 1967), pp. 58–9 (italics mine).
    For a contemporary account that merges the concepts 'person' and 'life' into the concept of a 'person life', see Marya Schechtman, *Staying Alive: Personal Identity, Practical Concerns, and the Unity of a Life* (Oxford: Oxford University Press, 2014).

38 *'with a strict care for the truth ...'*: André Maurois, *Aspects of Biography* (Cambridge: Cambridge University Press, 1929), p. 92. He adds that poetic truth demands 'artistic divination' – an intuitive knowledge that discerns recurrent 'motifs', even aesthetic 'unity'. W. H. Dunn had already enumerated the features of a good biography: it will be unified, coherent, selective, concentrated, brief and self-effacing; 'in short ... a work of art' – *English Biography* (London: J. M. Dent & Sons, 1916), p. 286.

38 *As Maurois discovered, life writing turns out to be a rather elastic genre*: Dunn's *English Biography* traces the evolution of this idea: 'More and more, as the [nineteenth] century drew near its close, did the conviction deepen that the great biography is a work of art, a created, a "fictive" thing ... hence arises the necessity of the biographer's being also an artist, and of the public's conceding to him the freedom to work as an

...   artist ... The line between truth and fiction in life narrative is perilously shadowy' (pp. 193–4).

41   *Every path is some combination of finding and making*: The question of how finding and making might be combined in writing a life underpins recent philosophical debates on 'narrativity'. Critics of narrative form, such as Galen Strawson, Hayden White and Jean-Paul Sartre, emphasize brute facts or pure experience (i.e. finding) onto which a narrative interpretation is imposed (i.e. making). Drawing on a hermeneutic tradition developed by Paul Ricoeur, Hans-Georg Gadamer and Charles Taylor, the literary theorist Hanna Meretoja has argued, against 'antinarrativist' philosophers, that 'we are always already entangled in stories and we constantly reinterpret our experiences through them' – see 'On the Use and Abuse of Narrative for Life: Towards an Ethics of Storytelling' in *Life and Narrative: The Risks and Responsibilities of Storying Experience*, eds Brian Schiff, Elizabeth McKim and Sylvie Patron (Oxford: Oxford University Press, 2017). Philosopher Marya Schechtman has contributed to these debates by drawing on a passage in *Middlemarch* to explore our 'dual perspective' as selves in time, at once ongoing and momentary – see 'Glad It Happened: Personal Identity and Ethical Depth', *Journal of Consciousness Studies*, vol. 27, nos 7–8 (2020), pp. 95–114.

41   *Yet our experience continually folds back and loops forward* ...: See Martin Heidegger, *Being and Time*, trans. John Macquarrie and Edward Robinson (New York, NY: Harper and Row, 1962), on the looping, 'ecstatic' movement of human temporality (pp. 377, 385–400); Hans Loewald, *Psychoanalysis and the History of the Individual* (New Haven, CT: Yale University Press, 1978), on 'human time' as 'an interpenetration and reciprocal relatedness of past, present and future' (pp. 22–3).

42   *'under the aspect of eternity'*: Spinoza, *Ethics* V, P29, scholium.

42   *'I am glad that I have been told this story and will remember it in the hour of need* ...': Karen Blixen, *Out of Africa* (London: Penguin, 1954), p. 215.

44   *which inspired Elena Ferrante's Neapolitan novels.* See Elena Ferrante, *In the Margins: On the Pleasures of Reading and Writing* (London: Europa Editions, 2022), pp. 54–61.

44   *'the "who", which appears so clearly and unmistakably to others, remains hidden from the person himself* ...': Hannah Arendt, *The Human Condition*, second edition. (Chicago: University of Chicago Press, 1998), pp. 179–80.

44   'To be alive means to live in a world that preceded one's own arrival and will
      survive one's departure ...': Arendt, *The Life of the Mind*, p. 20.

44   'for millennia, philosophy has diverted its gaze from the appearance of human
      beings ...': Adriana Cavarero, '*Who* Engenders Politics?', in *Italian
      Feminist Theory and Practice*, eds Graziella Parati and Rebecca West
      (London: Associated University Presses, 2002), pp. 88–103, p. 94.
      The second half of Cavarero's sentence is a quotation from Arendt,
      who explained in her Gifford Lectures that Hegel thought 'the highest
      function of philosophy ... is to eliminate the contingent,' and therefore
      he constructed a philosophical system that 'transforms all [particulars]
      into thought-beings and thus eliminates their most scandalous
      property, their realness, together with their contingency' – *The Life of
      the Mind*, p. 91. See also Cavarero, 'Narrative Against Destruction', *New
      Literary History*, vol. 46, no. 1 (2015), pp. 1–16.

45   'Unlike philosophy, which ... has persisted in capturing the universal in the
      trap of definition ...': Cavarero, *Relating Narratives* (London: Routledge,
      2000), p. 3.

46   'Narratives are an aid to thinking through certain philosophical issues ...':
      Eleonore Stump, 'Faith and the Problem of Evil' in *Seeking
      Understanding: The Stob Lectures, 1986–1998* (Grand Rapids, MI:
      Eerdmans, 2001), p. 511.

46   'the biographer's duty, like that of Wittgenstein's philosopher, is to resist
      the "craving for generality" characteristic of those who aspire to science':
      Ray Monk, 'Life Without Theory: Biography as an Exemplar of
      Philosophical Understanding', *Poetics Today*, vol. 28, no. 3 (2007),
      pp. 527–70; see Wittgenstein's *Philosophical Investigations* Part 1, §66,
      §109, §122. A similar conception of philosophy underpins the synthesis
      of literature and philosophy in the work of Cora Diamond and Martha
      Nussbaum: see Diamond, 'Having a Rough Story about what Moral
      Philosophy Is', *New Literary History*, vol. 15, no. 1 (1983) pp. 155–69, and
      Nussbaum, 'Love's Knowledge' in *Love's Knowledge: Essays on Philosophy
      and Literature*.

46   *biography only brings into sharper focus a concept of life-as-a-whole that
      already hovers on the horizon of our experience*: Biography may even
      help us to delineate the concept of a whole life: to put it in technical
      terms, we specify X's life-as-a-whole as the truthmaker, or the set of
      truthmakers, for any possible biography of X. 'Truthmaker' is a concept
      used by contemporary philosophers to denote some existing entity
      that accounts for the truth of a true proposition. Just as the world itself
      would be the truthmaker for 'a comprehensive "book of the world" that

... showed how all the truths about the world related to one another vis à vis what is fundamental and derivative', so a whole life would be the truthmaker (or set of truthmakers) for a comprehensive 'book' of that life – see Jamin Asay, 'Run Aground: Kit Fine's Critique of Truthmaker Theory', *The Philosophical Quarterly*, vol. 67, no. 268 (2017), pp. 443–63.

47 *'the mystery of the authentic I which lies behind our actual life'*: José Ortega y Gasset, 'In Search of Goethe from within' in *The Dehumanization of Art and Other Essays on Art, Culture, and Literature* (Princeton, NJ: Princeton University Press, 1968), pp. 144, 149.

48 *'enigmatic and remote, yet intense'*: Etienne Souriau, 'On the mode of existence of the work to be made' in *The Different Modes of Existence*, trans. Erik Beranek and Tim Howles (Minneapolis, MN: Univocal, 2015), p. 226.

48 *'The work's call is a bit like the call of the child ...'*: Souriau, 'On the Mode of Existence of the Work to Be Made', p. 235.

49 *'Everyone knows the work's call ... because everyone has had to answer to it'*: Souriau, 'On the Mode of Existence of the Work to Be Made', p. 235.

51 *a human life has an exhibitive, expressive quality*: See Arendt, *The Human Condition*: 'By acting and speaking, men show who they are, reveal actively their unique personal identity and thus make their appearance in the human world, while their physical identities appear without any activity of their own in the unique shape of the body and sound of the voice' (p. 179).

52 *'an existence'; 'singular but also merged with the movements of a generation'*: Annie Ernaux, *The Years*, trans. Alison L. Strayer (London: Fitzcarraldo Editions, 2017): 'She would like to reassemble these multiple images of herself, separate and discordant, thread them together with the story of her existence, starting with her birth during World War II up until the present day. Therefore, an existence that is singular but also merged with the movements of a generation. Each time she begins, she meets the same obstacles: how to represent the passage of historical time, the changing of things, ideas, and manners, and the private life of this woman? ... Her main concern is the choice between "I" and "she"' (pp. 167, 169).

53 *buried, like George Eliot's love letters*: The letters exchanged between George Eliot and her partner, George Henry Lewes, were buried with Eliot in Highgate Cemetery.

53   *an excess of detail can thwart the attempt to grasp a life in its wholeness and
      reveal its singular shape*: See W. H. Dunn's critique of Thomas Moore's
      voluminous biography of Byron in *English Biography*, pp. 181–2, and
      Maurois, *Aspects of Biography*, pp. 55–6.

53   *each life makes a unique pattern of diffusions*: See Cavarero, *Relating
      Narratives*: 'the etymological root that the terms *uniqueness* and *unity*
      share does not flatten them out in a homogenous substance, but rather
      renders them signs of an existence whose life-story is different from
      all others precisely because it is constitutively interwoven with many
      others' (p. 71).

54   *a Spinozist way of thinking about human goodness that contrasts with
      the Utilitarian and Kantian ethics ascendant during her own lifetime*:
      See Spinoza, *Ethics* IV, Preface, where Spinoza (in George Eliot's
      translation) discusses the ideal 'exemplar of human nature' that models
      goodness (pp. 227–8), a concept linked to imagined 'archetypes'
      (p. 226) – a word Eliot introduced to gloss 'model' as a translation for
      exemplaria (see p. 327). In *Janet's Repentance* George Eliot pointedly
      criticizes Utilitarianism – see *Scenes of Clerical Life*, vol. 2 (Edinburgh
      and London: William Blackwood and Sons, 1878), pp. 253–4; in *The
      Mill on the Floss* (Edinburgh and London: William Blackwood and
      Sons, 1878) she insists that 'the mysterious complexity of our life is not
      to be embraced by maxims' (vol. 3, p. 265).

55   *moral concepts such as law, imperative and obligation generate a rhetoric of
      violation and transgression, of blame and criticism, that fosters violence*: See
      Akeel Bilgrami, *Secularism, Identity and Enchantment* (Cambridge, MA:
      Harvard University Press, 2014), chapter 4. This point is also indebted
      to my conversations with Bilgrami.

55   *'it merits the devotion of our toil and of our emotions. The cult of the hero is as
      old as mankind ...'*: Maurois, *Aspects of Biography*, p. 183.

55   *'andres epiphanies, men who are fully manifest'*: Arendt, *The Life of the
      Mind*, p. 72.

55   *Kierkegaard notes that even a celebrated 'hero' such as Abraham needs
      his 'poet' to keep him visible in the world*: See S. Kierkegaard, *Fear and
      Trembling*, trans. C. Stephen Evans and Sylvia Walsh (Cambridge:
      Cambridge University Press, 2006), pp. 12–13.

56   *'Their spirit diffuses itself ... this is the key to the power of the greatest men'*:
      Ralph Waldo Emerson, *Representative Men* (Boston, MA: Phillips,
      Sampson & Co., 1850), p. 38. Emerson's six representative men are

...   Plato, Swedenborg, Montaigne, Shakespeare, Napoleon and Goethe. Carlyle's principal heroes are the Norse god Odin, the Prophet Mohammed, Dante, Shakespeare, Martin Luther, John Knox, Samuel Johnson, Rousseau, Robert Burns, Oliver Cromwell and Napoleon. Comte's positivist calendar divides the year into thirteen lunar months named after Moses, Homer, Aristotle, Archimedes, Caesar, St Paul, Charlemagne, Dante, Gutenberg, Shakespeare, Descartes, Frederick II and Bichat.

56   *to 'cut herself off', as a contemporary critic put it, 'from the splendid effects of Scott* ...: James Sully, 'George Eliot's Art', *Mind*, vol. 6, no. 23 (1881), pp. 379–80.

56   *'See how diffusive your one little life may be'*: The George Eliot Letters, vol. 5, ed. Gordon Haight (Oxford University Press, 1954–1978), p. 83.

56   *the best exemplars are not elite, exceptional heroes but, on the contrary, those who embody a good that can be shared by all*: See Spinoza, *Ethics* IV, P36 and P37.

59   *Deleuze even claimed that philosophy consists in creating concepts*: See Gilles Deleuze and Félix Guattari, *What Is Philosophy?*, trans. Hugh Tomlinson and Graham Burchell (New York, NY: Columbia University Press, 1994), pp. 5–12.

60   *Influential philosophers in both Indian and European traditions have conceived their work as therapeutic*: See *Philosophy as Therapeia: Perspectives from India and Europe,* eds Clare Carlisle and Jonardon Ganeri (Cambridge: Cambridge University Press, 2010).

60   *language is 'the house of being'*: Martin Heidegger, 'Letter on Humanism', trans. Frank A. Capuzzi, in *Pathmarks*, ed. William McNeill (Cambridge: Cambridge University Press, 1998), p. 239.

60   *The ancient Greek word* kosmos, *meaning order, arrangement or adornment, had a quotidian sense, like setting a table for dinner, or it could be applied to the whole universe*: See Andrea Nightingale, *Philosophy and Religion in Plato's Dialogues* (Cambridge: Cambridge University Press, 2021), pp. 213–61.

60   *In the* Timaeus, *Plato portrays philosophy as cosmic exegesis*: See Myles Burnyeat, *Explorations in Ancient and Modern Philosophy*, vol. 4 (Cambridge: Cambridge University Press, 2022), pp. 265–85; Nightingale, *Philosophy and Religion in Plato's Dialogues,* pp. 222–4. Burnyeat explains that in ancient Greece an 'exegetai' was someone

... who expounded an oracle or explained a dream, or a guide who took you round a temple or sanctuary; 'it would not be inappropriate to think of Timaeus as our guide to the beautiful design of the cosmos we inhabit' (p. 271).

60 *Putting things in order renders them more intelligible, and also more beautiful*: See Plato's *Gorgias*, 503e-506e; Barney, 'Plato on the *Kalon* and the Good', p. 365.

61 *we know a thing by knowing its causes*: See Spinoza, *Ethics* I, A4: 'the knowledge of an effect depends on, and implies, the knowledge of its cause.'

62 *'a basic category of contemporary thought'; 'a universal and obligatory means of registering the experience and existence of living things'*: Georges Canguilhem, 'The Living and Its Milieu', trans. John Savage, *Grey Room* no. 3 (spring 2001) pp. 7–31. Canguilhem wanted to explore this concept's 'potential richness for a philosophy of nature that focuses on the problem of individuality.' For in-depth discussions, see https://histanthro.org/tag/milieu.

63 *the 'baby-and-mother cosmos'*: See Jonathan Lear's introduction to *The Essential Loewald: Collected Papers and Monographs* (Hagerstown, MD: University Publishing Group, 2000): 'there is first a baby-and-mother cosmos that is relatively undifferentiated. And then through the workings of love *within* that cosmos, an infant and mother differentiate out and together constitute a more complex world in which two more differentiated entities stand in essential relations to one another' (p. xxviii).

63 *This transition is paradigmatically ambiguous*: See Hans Loewald, 'The Ego and Reality', *International Journal of Psychoanalysis*, vol. 32 (1951), pp. 16–17; 'Transference and Love', in *Psychoanalysis and the History of the Individual*, pp. 29–51, especially pp. 36–9, 45–6. Loewald theorizes this passage as a transition from 'narcissistic libido' to 'oedipal phase' – a transition that is never fully accomplished.

63 *Most cultures contain vivid emblems of the maternal milieu*: See Erich Neumann, *The Great Mother: An Analysis of the Archetype*, trans. Ralph Manheim (London: Routledge and Kegan Paul, 1955).

64 *For Goldstein, the relationship between a living being and its 'continuously forming' milieu is like a dialogue* ...: Kurt Goldstein argued that each organism seeks to creates for itself an 'adequate milieu' within the 'world' comprising the sum of its surrounding conditions. This milieu

...   is 'by no means something definite and static, but is continuously forming commensurably with the development of the organism and its activity' – *The Organism: A Holistic Approach to Biology Derived from Pathological Data in Man*, trans. Heinz Anbacher et al. (New York, NY: American Book Company, 1939), p. 88.

64   *both physical and mental relations 'between every organism and the external world'*: Herbert Spencer, *Principles of Psychology* (London: Longman, Brown, Green and Longmans, 1855), pp. 374–9. Here Spencer defines 'life' as 'the continuous adjustment of internal relations to external relations.'

65   *'For does not society modify Man, according to the conditions [les milieux] in which he lives and acts ...'; 'Man has a tendency to express [à représenter] his culture, his thoughts, and his life in everything he appropriates to his use'*: Honoré de Balzac, *La Comédie humaine*, vol. 1 (Paris: Louis Conard, 1912), pp. xxvi–xvii.

65   *Proust believed that Balzac's readers 'came to see a sort of literary quality in a hundred everyday occurrences'*: Marcel Proust, *By Way of Sainte-Beuve*, trans. Sylvia Townsend Warner (London: Chatto & Windus, 1958), p. 138.

65   *'reading enhances the value of life, a value we have not realised until books make us aware of how great that value is'*: Marcel Proust, *Time Regained*, trans. Stephen Hudson (London: Chatto & Windus, 1960), p. 30.

65   *'air of lucidity ...'*: Eve Babitz, 'The Hollywood Branch Library' in *Eve's Hollywood* (New York: New York Review Books, 2015), pp. 230–37.

65   *'in her book she would like to save everything that has continually been around her. She wants to save her circumstance... She will go within herself only to retrieve the world'*: Ernaux, *The Years*, pp. 190, 222, 225.

66   *'a common time'*: Ernaux, *The Years*, p. 222.

66   *a sense of ourselves as self-contained subjectivities set apart from the world, and thus able to have a 'view' or 'picture' of it ...*: See Clifford Geertz, 'Ethos, World View and the Analysis of Sacred Symbols', *The Antioch Review*, vol. 17, no. 4 (1957), pp. 622–37.

67   *it embodies and articulates its specific milieu: the materials it was made from, the crafts and technologies used to produce it, the ways it is (or was) engaged with or put to use*: See John Tresch, *Cosmograms: How To Do Things With Worlds* (Chicago, IL: University of Chicago Press, forthcoming).

67   *Heidegger asked this question of Van Gogh's painting of a pair of old boots*:
       See Martin Heidegger, 'The Origin of the Work of Art' in *Martin
       Heidegger: Basic Writings*, ed. David Farrell Krell (San Francisco:
       Harper, 1993), pp. 143–203.

69   *a human self is a synthesis of necessity and possibility*: See S. Kierkegaard,
       The Sickness unto Death, trans. Edna H. Hong and Howard V. Hong
       (Princeton, NJ: Princeton University Press, 1983), pp. 29–42.

69   *He likened possibility to oxygen; without it, we feel 'unable to breathe',
       spiritually suffocated*: See Kierkegaard, *The Sickness Unto Death*, pp.
       38–9.

69   *'an imagined otherwise', 'I sometimes wonder what my life had been /
       Without that voice as channel to my soul'*: See George Eliot, *Middlemarch*
       (Edinburgh and London: William Blackwood and Sons, 1878), vol. 2,
       p. 297 and 'Armgart' in *The Legend of Jubal and Other Poems, Old and New*
       (Edinburgh and London: William Blackwood and Sons, 1878), pp. 75–
       6; Barbara Hardy, *The Novels of George Eliot* (London: Athlone Press,
       1959), pp. 135–54; Debra Gettelman, *Imagining Otherwise* (Princeton,
       NJ: Princeton University Press, 2024).

69   *Eliot once described this literary process as a passage to 'the irrevocable'*: *The
       George Eliot Letters*, vol. 6, p. 91.

70   *'living mirrors or images of the universe'*: G. W. Leibniz, *Monadology* §83.

70   *While autobiography depicts this meaning-making with a 'special intimacy
       of understanding', a biographer, Dilthey argued, has the privilege of seeing
       the whole of a life ...*: Wilhelm Dilthey, *Selected Works*, vol. 3 (Princeton,
       NJ: Princeton University Press, 2002), p. 221. Like Cavarero, Dilthey
       believed that a biographer has a chance of understanding a person
       better than she understood herself – see H. P. Rickman, 'Wilhelm
       Dilthey and Biography', *Biography*, vol. 2, no. 3 (1979), pp. 218–229.

71   *This milieu shaped Schleiermacher's life, and this particular life discloses
       the milieu*: An individual, wrote Dilthey, 'dwells in the sphere of the
       state, religion, or science – in brief, in a distinctive life-system or in
       a constellation of them. The inner structure of such a constellation
       draws the individual into it, shapes him, and determines the direction
       of his productivity. Historical achievements stem from the possibilities
       inherent in the inner structure of an historical moment' – Dilthey,
       Selected Works, vol. 3, pp. 266–7.

71   *'significant individual'*: Dilthey, *Selected Works*, vol. 2 (Princeton, NJ:

...   Princeton University Press, 2010), p. 6.

71   *'A human being carries a whole epoch within him, just as a wave carries the whole of the sea'*: See Paul Crittenden, 'The Singular Universal in Jean-Paul Sartre', *Literature and Aesthetics*, vol. 8 (1998). Also: each human life is 'a singular embodiment of the ongoing totalization that envelops and produces it' – Jean-Paul Sartre, 'The Singular Universal' in *Between Existentialism and Marxism*, trans. John Mathews (New York: Pantheon Book, 1975), pp. 141–69.

72   *'a lighted candle as a centre of illumination ...'*: George Eliot, *Middlemarch*, vol. 1, p. 403.

72   *'but a set of relations selected and combined ...?'*: George Eliot, 'Notes on Form in Art' in *The Essays of George Eliot*, ed. Thomas Pinney (London: Routledge and Kegan Paul, 1963), pp. 431–6.

73   *'refashioning her little world into just what she should like it to be'*: George Eliot, *The Mill on the Floss*, vol. 1, p. 69.

73   *'the petty medium of Middlemarch'* is *'too strong for him'*: George Eliot, *Middlemarch*, vol. 1, p. 285.

73   *'hard and unkind'*: George Eliot, *The Mill on the Floss*, vol. 2, p. 80.

76   *'I at least have so much to do in unravelling certain human lots ...'*: George Eliot, *Middlemarch*, vol. 1, p. 214.

77   *At the core of this novel is the relationship between what is ordinary and trivial, and what is great and significant*: Eliot had read several of Balzac's novels, and may have been influenced by his manifesto in the preface to the *Comédie humaine*: 'I attach to common, everyday facts, hidden or patent, to the acts of individual lives, to their causes and principles, the importance which historians have hitherto ascribed to the events of national public life' (p. xxxv).

77   *'There would be nothing trivial about our lives ...'*: George Eliot, *Middlemarch*, vol. 1, p. 40.

77   *'chosen to fulfil a great destiny, entailing a terribly different experience from that of ordinary womanhood'*: John Cross, *George Eliot's Life, as Related in Her Letters and Journals*, vol. 3 (Cambridge: Cambridge University Press, 2010), pp. 42–4 (from Eliot's notes on her verse drama *The Spanish Gypsy*).

78   *Here the action unfolds in an explicitly cosmic milieu* ...: See the epigram to
       Chapter 16 of *Daniel Deronda*.

78   *'chooses a companion soul of better fortune and more strength'*: *George Eliot's
       Daniel Deronda Notebooks*, ed. Jane Irwin (Cambridge: Cambridge
       University Press, 1996), p. 455.

78   *'Individuals in the lower world ... have their types in the higher, so that
       nothing here is trivial, but all has a higher significance ...'*: *George Eliot's
       Daniel Deronda Notebooks*, pp. 173–4.

79   *'lost amongst millions of worlds'*; *'every fixed sun is a star, which diffuses light
       to its surrounding worlds'*: Bernard le Bovier de Fontenelle, *Conversations
       on the Plurality of Worlds*, trans. Elizabeth Gunning, ed. Jerome de la
       Lande (London: T. Hurst and T. Ostell, 1803), pp. 110–13.

79   *'Yes ... I only ask as a reward for my trouble, that whenever you see the sun, the
       skies, the stars, you think of me'*: Fontenelle, *Conversations on the Plurality
       of Worlds*, p. 131.

81   *'Your one little life'*: See note to p. 56.

84   *'You are the light of the world ...'*: See John 1:9; Matthew 5.

85   *'in letting his own light shine, led his disciples to hope that they would
       attain to such excellence by imitating him'*: Xenophon, *Memorabilia* 1.2.3.
       Another example: Jesus identifies himself with anyone who is in need:
       hungry, thirsty, naked, sick, imprisoned, foreign or homeless (see
       Matthew 25:31–46). And the test is not whether people have recognized
       him to be the Son of God, but whether they have looked after those
       who needed help and care. Yet when his disciples try to apply this
       teaching, by objecting to a woman who pours expensive perfumed oil
       over his head – that could have been sold, they say, and the proceeds
       given to the poor – Jesus praises the woman's gesture: it is a sign of her
       faith in him (see Matthew 26:6–13). John's gospel depicts this scene as
       happening at the home of Lazarus, Mary and Martha. In this version it
       is Mary who pours the perfumed oil on Jesus's feet, and it is the disciple
       Judas Iscariot, Jesus's betrayer, who asks why the oil wasn't sold to help
       the poor. The contrast here is between faithful Mary and treacherous
       Judas.

85   *'the only Son of God'*: See, e.g., the Nicene Creed and the Apostles'
       Creed.

85   *'perceived things truly and accurately'*: See chapter 4 of Spinoza's

...   *Theologico-Political Treatise*, in *The Collected Works of Spinoza*, vol. 2, pp. 132–3; Carlisle, *Spinoza's Religion: A New Reading of the Ethics*, p. 109.

85   *'In this sense ... we can say that God's Wisdom, that is, a Wisdom surpassing human wisdom, assumed a human nature in Christ, and that Christ was a way to salvation* [et Christum viam salutis fuisse]': See chapter 1 of Spinoza's *Theologico-Political Treatise*, in *The Collected Works of Spinoza* vol. 2, ed. Edwin Curley (Princeton, NJ: Princeton University Press, 2016), pp. 84–5. Spinoza concludes these remarks by distancing himself from Christian orthodoxy: 'I must warn here that I'm not speaking in any way about the things some of the Churches maintain about Christ. Not that I deny them. For I readily confess I don't grasp them.'

85   *'clarify and soften the things in the* Theologico-Political Treatise *which caused trouble to your Readers'*: See *The Collected Works of Spinoza*, vol. 2, p. 464 (Letter 71, Henry Oldenburg to Benedict de Spinoza, 15 November 1675).

85   *'We must think quite differently about the eternal son of God, i.e., God's eternal wisdom, which has manifested itself in all things and chiefly in the human mind, and most of all in Jesus Christ'*: See *The Collected Works of Spinoza*, vol. 2, p. 468 (Letter 73, Benedict de Spinoza to Henry Oldenburg, 15 December 1675).

86   *'the Christian word* incarnation'; *'in all religions incarnations are known'*: Adam Gifford, 'The Ten Avatars of Vishnu', p. 130.

87   *When Goethe and the German Romantics took up Spinozism, they emphasized that human beings channel the creative power of God or Nature*: Spinoza drew a conceptual distinction between 'natured nature' (*natura naturata*) and 'naturing nature' (*natura naturans*) – between nature that is made or caused, and nature that is productive, poetic. For the Romantics we are most importantly part of nature in the productive, poetic sense.

87   *'full of grace and philosophy'*; *'passed like clouds round the foot of that mountain, on the summit of which his genius is placed'*: See Madame de Staël, *De l'Allemagne* (Paris: Libraire de Firmin Didot Frères, 1853), p. 128.

87   *the question for each individual was whether they reacted with offence or faith when confronted with the paradox of Christ as divine incarnation*: See S. Kierkegaard, *Philosophical Fragments*, trans. Edna H. Hong and Howard V. Hong (Princeton, NJ: Princeton University Press, 1985)

...   and *Practice in Christianity*, trans. Edna H. Hong and Howard V. Hong (Princeton, NJ: Princeton University Press, 1991).

89   'considered herself a revelation of the mind of the Deity': George Eliot's *Letters*, vol. 1, p. 162 (Mary Sibree to John Sibree, 6 March 1843). Spinoza wrote that 'God's eternal word and covenant and true religion are divinely inscribed upon the hearts of men, that is, upon the human mind': see Spinoza's *Theologico-Political Treatise*, chapter 12 in *The Collected Works of Spinoza*, vol. 2, p. 248.

91   'suppressed experience': see George Eliot, *Daniel Deronda* (Edinburgh and London: William Blackwood and Sons, 1878), p. 120.

92   *While Diana, like Gwendolen, surely has her demonic side ...*: Hans Loewald defines 'daemonic' 'as in the Greek idea of *daemon*, neither attributable to the power of a personal god, nor a powerful force of the person *qua* individual or conscious being, but something in between, having an impersonal character' – *Psychoanalysis and the History of the Individual*, p. 9. Here Loewald is discussing Freudian theory, suggesting that 'there is something daemonic about the id.'

92   *People described her as radiant or dazzling; they recognized that* kalon *quality as soon as they saw it*: Gabriel Richardson Lear discusses the radiance of the *kalon* in 'Plato on Why Human Beauty is Good for the Soul', *Oxford Studies in Ancient Philosophy*, vol. 57 (Oxford: Oxford University Press, 2020).

94   'A sky as vast as ours could ... be formed from a quantity of matter which might be held in the hollow of the hand': John Tyndall, 'The Scientific Use of the Imagination' (London: Longmans, Green & Co., 1870), pp. 25–6.

94   'What in the midst of that mighty drama are girls and their blind visions?'; 'Could there be a slenderer, more insignificant thread in human history than this consciousness of a girl ...?': George Eliot, *Daniel Deronda*, vol. 2, p. 181.

95   *a 'vessel' containing 'all the wondrous combinations of the universe'*: See George Eliot, *Daniel Deronda*, vol. 2, p. 182.

95   Daniel Deronda *depicts a decadent Christian establishment complicit in the brutalities of Empire*: The novel's worldly Anglican priest, Mr Gascoigne, colludes with the corruption and violence personified by Gwendolen's wealthy husband – the sort of 'white-handed man' who would be esteemed for his capacity for cruelty (indeed, for

...   'extermination') if he were 'sent to govern a difficult colony'. See vol. 3, p. 74.

98   'Natura naturans *and* Natura naturata *are one and the same* ...': Romain Rolland, *Le Voyage intérieur* (Paris: Editions Albin Michel, 1959), pp. 36–7.

98   *'past and future meld into one, as into an eternal present....'*: *Cahiers Romain Rolland*, vol. 4 (Paris: Éditions Albin Michel, 1952), pp. 77, 359. See William Parsons, *The Enigma of the Oceanic Feeling* (Oxford: Oxford University Press, 1999), pp. 94–6; Henri Vermorel, 'The Presence of Spinoza in the Exchanges Between Sigmund Freud and Romain Rolland', *International Journal of Psychoanalysis*, vol. 90, no. 6 (2009), pp. 1235–54.

99   *'caused me no small difficulty* ...': Sigmund Freud, 'Civilization and its Discontents' in *The Standard Edition of the Complete Psychological Works of Sigmund Freud, Volume XXI (1927–1931)*, ed. James Strachey (London: Vintage Random House, 2001).

99   *The dialogue between Rolland and Freud, and the ideas it generated on both sides, would shape debates* ...: See Loewald, 'Some Comments on Religious Experience' in *Psychoanalysis and the History of the Individual*, pp. 55–77; Parsons, *The Enigma of the Oceanic Feeling*.

99   'Ramakrishna lies very near to my heart ...': Romain Rolland, *The Life of Ramakrishna*, trans. E. F. Malcolm-Smith (Mayavati: Advaita Ashram, 1930), pp. 1–2.

100   *'very current in the East Indies'* ...: Pierre Bayle, *Dictionnaire historique et critique de Pierre Bayle, Nouvelle Edition, Tome treizième* (Paris: Desoer, 1820), pp. 424–5. Bayle relies on the account of Hinduism presented in François Bernier's 1668 'Letter to M. Chapelain on the Superstitions, Strange Customs and Doctrines of the Hindus [*Indous*] or Gentiles of Hindustan.'

100   *Coleridge described Spinoza as 'the sternest and most consistent of the Adwitamists'*: See K. G. Srivastava, *Bhagavad Gītā und the English Romantic Movement* (New Delhi: Macmillan India, 2002), p. 209; Jonardon Ganeri, 'Cosmic Consciousness', *The Monist* no. 105 (2002), pp. 43–57. Indian scholars later developed the comparison between Spinozism and Advaita Vedānta in some detail: see Maganlal A. Buch, *The Philosophy of Shankara* (Baroda: Vidya Vilas Press, 1921), Rama Kanta Tripathi, *Spinoza in the Light of the Vedānta* (Varanasi: Bhargava Bhushan Press, 1957) and Bina Gupta, 'Brahman, God, Substance and

...   Nature: Samkara and Spinoza', *Indian Philosophical Quarterly*, vol. 11, no. 3 (1984), pp. 265–83.

100   *Herder's devotional response to Indian art, religion and philosophy shaped the mythical image of India in German Romanticism* ...: See A. Leslie Willson, 'Herder and India: The Genesis of a Mythical Image', *PMLA*, vol. 70, no. 5 (1955), pp. 1049–58; Johann Gottfried Herder, *God: Some Conversations*, trans. Frederick Henry Burkhardt (New York: Veritas Press, 1940).

101   *'Brahman, as conceived in the Upanishads and defined by Śankara, is clearly the same as Spinoza's* Substantia': F. Max Müller, *Three Lectures on the Vedānta Philosophy, delivered at the Royal Institution in March, 1894* (London: Longmans, Green & Co., 1894), p. 123. See also the preface to the fourth edition of Monier Monier-Williams's *Brahmanism and Hinduism; or, Religious Thought and Life in India* (New York: Macmillan, 1891): 'Hinduism is founded on that highly subtle theory of pantheistic philosophy ... if I may be allowed the anachronism, the Hindus were Spinozaites more than 2000 years before the existence of Spinoza' (p. xii).

101   *His book,* De Open-Deure tot het Verborgen Heydendom *(The Open Door to Hidden Paganism) was soon translated into French and German, and became an important source for Herder*: See A. Leslie Willson, 'Rogerius' "Open-Deure": A Herder Source', *Monatshefte*, vol. 24, no. 1 (1956), pp. 17–24.

101   *the ten avatars of Vishnu and south India's five principal Śiva shrines* ...: See Abraham Rogerius, *De Open-Deure tot het Verborgen Heydendom*, ed. W. Caland (Leiden: Martinus Nijhoff, 1915), pp. 112–14.

101   *Its author recommends renouncing worldly things and retreating to a mountain cave* ...: See *Bhartrihari: Poems*, trans. Barbara Stoler Miller (New York: Columbia University Press, 1967), pp. 9, 123–5, 131, 139, 141, 145, 147.

103   *Over the next few years an ashram gradually took shape around him* ...: See Sri Annamalai Swami, *Living By the Words of Bhagavan*, trans. Sundaram Swami and ed. David Godman (Tiruvannamalai: Sri Annamalai Swami Ashram Trust, 1994), p. 40. Here Ramana's attendant Annamalai Swami describes how Ramana moved into a small room built over his mother's tomb a few months after her death in 1922; the meditation hall was completed around 1927–8.

103   *'mystical state of consciousness'*: See William James, *The Varieties of*

...   *Religious Experience* (New York: Random House, 1902), especially Lecture 16 on 'Mysticism'. James defined mystical states according to four criteria – ineffability; noetic quality; transiency; passivity – and explained that they 'modify the inner life of the subject' (pp. 371–2). On 'transformative experience' as a concept applied to Ramana's life, see e.g. Thomas A. Forsthoefel, 'Weaving the Inward Thread to Awakening: The Perennial Appeal of Ramana Maharshi', *Horizons*, vol. 29, no. 2 (2002), p. 246. For a philosophical analysis of the concept, see L. A. Paul, *Transformative Experience* (Oxford: Oxford University Press, 2014).

104   *'This body is going to die, I said to myself...'*: See 'The Death Experience of Bhagavan', *Mountain Path*, vol. 18, no. 2 (1981), pp. 67–9; David Godman, 'Bhagavan's Self-realisation' (https://www.davidgodman. org/bhagavans-self-realisation/).

104   *avesam, a Tamil word meaning possession by a spirit*: The concept of *avesam* implies a dualism between the spirit and the body it possesses; however, it resonates with the Sanskrit *avesa*, used to describe the finite self merging with Lord Śiva. Common to these two meanings is a release from ordinary agency. See Godman, 'Bhagavan's Self-realisation.'

104   *'The fact is, I did nothing....'*: See A. Devaraja Mudaliar, *Day by Day with Bhagavan: From the Diary of A. Devaraja Mudaliar* (Tiruvannamalai: Sri Ramana Ashram, 2002), p. 317 (4 October 1946).

105   *Here he 'trembled'*: See 'The Death Experience of Bhagavan', *Mountain Path*, vol. 18, no. 2 (1981), pp. 67–9.

105   *Yet before he left home he had never heard of Brahman ...*: See *The Teachings of Bhagavan Sri Ramana Maharshi in his Own Words*, ed. Arthur Osborne (London: Rider & Co., 1962), p. 11; 'The Death Experience of Bhagavan', p. 68.

107   *'in search of my father and in obedience to his command'*: See David Godman, 'An introduction to Sri Ramana's Life and Teachings' (https://www.davidgodman.org/an-introduction-to-sri-ramanas-life-and-teachings/).

107   *'burns the ego to destruction'*: See Michael James, 'The Power of Arunachala', *The Mountain Path*, vol. 19, no. 2 (1982), pp. 75–84.

107   *'is pure jnana in the form of a hill. It is out of compassion for those who seek him that Śiva has chosen to reveal himself in the form of a hill visible to the*

... *eye. The seeker will obtain guidance and solace by staying close to this hill*': James, 'The Power of Arunachala', quoting Dr. T. N. Krishnaswamy.

107 *describes the seeking soul as a bride and Lord Arunachala as its bridegroom, though it also addresses Arunachala as 'father' and 'mother'*: Sri Ramana Maharshi, 'Marital Garland of Letters' in *Five Hymns to Arunachala*, trans. K. Swaminathan (Tiruvannamalai: Sri Ramana Ashram, 2001), pp. 23, 36. Ramana wrote this first hymn on the request of his devotees who used to walk into Tiruvannamalai asking for alms: they wanted a distinctive song, so that people would recognize them as Ramana's devotees. By this time other alms-beggars were pretending to be from Ramana, because people gave more food for him than for other sadhus.

108 *'In Tiruchuzhi, the holy town of Bhuminatha ...'*: Sri Ramana Maharshi, 'Necklace of Nine Gems' in *Five Hymns to Arunachala*, pp. 106–11.

108 *'Look, there it stands as if insentient ...'*: Sri Ramana Maharshi, 'Arunachala Ashtakam' in *Five Hymns to Arunachala*, p. 121.

108 *'In order to reveal Yourself at last as Being and Awareness ...'*: Sri Ramana Maharshi, 'Arunachala Ashtakam' in *Five Hymns to Arunachala*, p. 123.

109 *'The raindrops showered down by the clouds ...'*: Sri Ramana Maharshi, 'Arunachala Ashtakam' in *Five Hymns to Arunachala*, p. 125.

109 *a legal deposition opposing the Indian government's plan to seize control of Arunachala and fell its trees*: See David Godman, 'Bhagavan's Deposition on Arunachala' (https://www.davidgodman.org/bhagavans-deposition-on-arunachala/). Ramana made his deposition in 1938, in support of the temple which sought to retain its legal rights over the south-eastern portion of the hill. The temple's claim was unsuccessful; the government seized control of Arunachala and its trees were felled. Yet Ramana's wishes were eventually fulfilled: the local forestry department together with a volunteer group led by a Ramana devotee have now restored trees and wildlife to Arunachala. During the planting season in 2024 Joseph and I carried a couple of saplings up the hill.

111 *He did not present or publicize himself as a teacher*: See Arthur Osborne, *My Life and Quest* (Tiruvannamalai: Sri Ramana Ashram, 2001), pp. 67, 85, 100–104.

111 *Q&A dialogues*: Especially significant is Sri Muruganar's *Guru Vachaka Kovai* (first edition 1939, second edition 1971). Muruganar, a poet, Tamil scholar and Ramana devotee, composed Tamil verses summarizing Ramana's verbal teachings in close collaboration with Ramana himself

...   – see *Guru Vachaka Kovai*, trans. T. V. Venkatasubramanian, Robert Butler and David Godman (Boulder, CO: Avadhuta Foundation, 2008), pp. xviii–xxvii.

111   '*is not attaining something new ...*': *Be As You Are: The Teachings of Sri Ramana Maharshi*, ed. David Godman (London: Arkana, 1985), pp. 12–14. This passage continues: 'When all of our [false notions and tendencies] have been given up, the Self will shine alone.' 'False notions and tendencies' translates *samskaras*: mental impressions, dispositions, impulses, recollections, psychological imprints that ... accumulate as a consequence of actions – see Ian Whicher, *The Integrity of the Yoga Darsana* (Albany, NY: SUNY Press, 1999), pp. 99–102.

111   '*You are to remain in your true state*': *The Teachings of Ramana Maharshi*, ed. Arthur Osborne (Tiruvannamalai: Sri Ramana Ashram, 1993), p. 96.

111   *Over time, 'Who am I?' would draw the questioner into inward contemplation* ...: See Arthur Osborne (ed.), *The Collected Works of Ramana Maharshi* (London: Rider & Co., 1959), p. 41; Ankur Barua, 'The Silences of Ramana Maharshi: Self-Enquiry and Realisation in Sāmkhya Yoga and Advaita Vedānta', *Religions of South Asia*, vol. 9, no. 2, pp. 186–207.

112   '*How do you know I am not doing it?* ...': Munagala Venkataramiah, *Talks with Sri Ramana Maharshi* (Tiruvannamalai: Sri Ramana Ashram, 2010), pp. 254–5; see also pp. 19, 76–7, 210, 252, 386, 439. Ramana also believed that spiritual teachings must differ according to the student's temperament and maturity, so that mass instruction would be ineffective and perhaps detrimental.

113   '*in search of the Yogis and their hermetic knowledge*': Paul Brunton, *A Search in Secret India* (London: Rider and Company, 1970), p. 19. Brunton was born Hyman Abraham Isaacs and changed his name to Raphael Hurst, then to Paul Brunton.

114   *The theosophists believed that ancient India possessed the highest wisdom – and that modern Europeans were best placed to recover it*: See H. P. Blavatsky, 'What Are the Theosophists?', *The Theosophist*, vol. 1, no. 1 (1879), pp. 5–7; *The Secret Doctrine*, vol. 2 (London: Theosophical Publishing, 1888), p. 301.

114   '*As a child of this modern generation* ...': Brunton, *A Search in Secret India*, p. 19.

114   *'He has strangely conquered me ...'*: Brunton, *A Search in Secret India*,
      pp. 311–12.

115   *eager not 'to shoot a tiger or to sell anything ... nor to see the Taj Mahal',*
      but to 'meet scholars, writers and artists, religious teachers and devotees':
      Somerset Maugham, 'The Saint' in *Points of View* (London:
      Heinemann, 1958), p. 56. Maugham gives the date of his India trip as
      1936; other sources say 1938.

116   *whose 'supreme achievement,' wrote Maugham, 'was to take the speculations*
      of the Upanishads ...': Maugham, 'The Saint', pp. 61–3. On Śankara
      and the *Vivekacudami* see *The Vivekacudamani of Śankaracarya*
      Bhagavatpada, ed. John Grimes (Delhi: Motilal Banarsidass, 2004),
      pp. 1–53: the *Vivekacudami*'s author is now thought to be a Kashmiri
      Śaiva scholar who lived 200 years after Śankara.
          Major A. W. Chadwick, an English devotee who lived in the
      ashram from 1935 until his death in 1962, disputes Maugham's
      account of sitting in the meditation hall with Ramana: according to
      Chadwick, he just looked into the hall through the window. Maugham
      did, however, meet Ramana face to face in Chadwick's own room.
      Suggested models for Larry Darrell, the protagonist of *The Razor's Edge*,
      include an American engineer named Guy Hague, the English novelist
      Christopher Isherwood and Paul Brunton – see David Godman,
      'Somerset Maugham and *The Razor's Edge*', *The Mountain Path*, vol. 12,
      no. 4 (1988), pp. 239–45.

116   *'At sunset he asked to be raised to a sitting position ...'*: Maugham, 'The
      Saint', p. 95. In fact the chanting began around 8 p.m. – after sunset –
      and Ramana Maharshi died at 8.47 p.m. Ramana's disciple Annamalai
      Swami described that evening as follows: 'At that moment I saw the
      great light in the sky, the light that signified that Bhagavan had died.
      Many people saw this light and most of them reported that it resembled
      a meteor. It appeared to me in a different form: I saw a great column
      of light about twenty feet high and 1½ feet wide in the middle of the
      sky. While it was manifesting for a period of about two minutes it was
      slowly descending towards the ashram. A few minutes later a *sādhu*
      came and told me that Bhagavan had passed away' – *Living by the Words*
      of Bhagavan, p. 212.

117   *He longed to go to India to see him ...*: See Maya Rauch, 'Heinrich Zimmer
      from a Daughter's Perspective' in *Heinrich Zimmer: Coming Into His*
      Own, ed. Margaret Case (Princeton, NJ: Princeton University Press,
      2017) pp. 19–20.

117   *To Zimmer's amazement, he had not, despite – or perhaps because of –*

... *Ramana's renown as a master of Self-realization, an ideal Jung also advocated*: The first time Zimmer met Jung, in 1932, he asked him what he thought 'about the Hindu idea of the transcendental Self, in-dwelling man, underlying his conscious personality as well as the vast depth of the unconscious including the archetypes' – see Henry R. Zimmer, 'The Impress of Dr Jung on My Profession' in *Heinrich Zimmer: Coming Into His Own*, pp. 43–4.

Jung's Foreword to Zimmer's Ramana book, *Der Weg zum Selbst* classified this 'holy man' as merely a 'type': 'Therefore it was not necessary to seek him out. I saw him all over India, in the pictures of Ramakrishna, in Ramakrishna's disciples, in Buddhist monks' – from 'The Holy Men of India' in *The Collected Works of C. G. Jung*, vol. 11, ed. Gerhard Adler and trans. R. F. C. Hull (Princeton, NJ: Princeton University Press, 1970), pp. 576–7. Reviewing *Der Weg zum Selbst* for an American journal, Joseph Campbell commended Zimmer's translation of Ramana's teachings yet criticized Jung's preface for trying to 'devaluate' both Indian philosophy and Ramana himself – see Margaret H. Case, 'Introduction' in *Heinrich Zimmer: Coming Into His Own*, p. 12.

On 'Self-realization', see *Letters of C. G. Jung, vol. 2, 1951–1961*, ed. Gerhard Adler (Princeton, NJ: Princeton University Press, 1976), p. 316, where Jung writes: 'We have become participants in the divine life and we have to assume a new responsibility, viz. the continuation of the divine self-realization, which expresses itself in the task of our individuation'; see also pp. 25, 146, 494. The culture surrounding Jungian analysis in the 1930s and '40s was more hierarchical and more classical than at Ramana's ashram: erudition was highly valued, and Jung's techniques for self-realization were transmitted via a process of analytic training resembling a traditional guru lineage. In *Feet of Clay: A Study of Gurus* (London: Harper Collins, 1996) psychiatrist Anthony Storr concludes that Jung 'certainly thought of himself as a spiritual leader' (p. 96).

118 *'India's ancient message': 'a message telling us to transcend the "I", to renounce the illusion of the world, to become a saviour full of redeeming knowledge'*: Heinrich Zimmer, 'Die Schale der Persönlichkeit' ('The Shell of Personality', Zimmer's introduction to his translation of the teachings of Ramana Maharshi), *Der Weg zum Selbst: Lehre und Leben des indischen Heiligen Shri Ramana Maharshi aus Tiruvannamalai* (Zurich: Rascher Verlag, 1954), p. 81.

118 *'She stepped into the hall where he used to sit ...'*: Osborne, *My Life and Quest*, pp. 70–71 (the published title differed from Osborne's original title, so as not to confuse it with *The Mountain Path*, the Ramana Ashram's journal, which Osborne founded in 1964).

119   *'religion can be replaced only by religion ...'*: See *The Freud-Jung Letters*, ed. William McGuire (Princeton University Press, 1974), p. 294 (Letter 178). Jung says here that he wants to 'revivify among intellectuals a feeling for symbol and myth.'

119   *Jung concluded that 'every one' of his European patients 'fell ill because he has lost what the living religions of every age have given to their followers ...'*: *The Collected Works of C. G. Jung*, vol. 11, p. 331.

120   *their enlightened 'tolerance' of 'non-Christian faiths'...*: See Ruth Harris, *Guru to the World: The Life and Legacy of Vivekananda* (Cambridge, MA: Belknap Press, 2022), pp. 2, 121–4, 136. Harris notes that naming the World's Fair a Columbian Exposition 'memorialized Christian conquest.'

120   *Japanese delegates rebuked missionary Christianity for 'devastating' and 'trampling' their nation 'under the disguise of religion', while Vivekananda, the charismatic star of India's delegation, announced that Hinduism had 'taught the world ... universal acceptance'*: See Harris, *Guru to the World*, pp. 126, 133.

120   *Local and national newspapers reported his striking claim that 'The Hindu refuses to call you sinners. Ye are the Children of God, the sharers of immortal bliss, holy and perfect beings'*: Harris, *Guru to the World*, pp. 133–5. Vivekananda presented Hindu universalism in explicit contrast with Christianity's claim that Christ is the only way to salvation (see John 14:6). His performance in Chicago made him famous in the West and initiated the spread of Yoga and Advaita Vedānta throughout North America. Back in India, young Ramana saw a copy of Vivekananda's Chicago lecture at his American high school, some time between 1893 and 1896. Around 1901, while Ramana was living in Virupaksha cave, his devotee Sri Gambhiram Seshayyar brought him Vivekananda's English lectures on Raja yoga and Jnana yoga, asking Ramana to explain them to him – see *The Mountain Path*, vol. 22, no. 4 (1985), p. 252.

121   *a 'jungle sage'*: Brunton, *A Search in Secret India*, p. 19. On jungle metaphors in European accounts of Hinduism, see Ronald Inden, *Imagining India* (Oxford: Blackwell, 1990), pp. 86–7.

121   *the eternal Self (Atman) is 'the common experience of all'*: See *Vivekachudamani of Sri Sankaracharya*, trans. Swami Madhavananda (Advaita Ashrama, Mayavati: Prabuddha Bharata Press, 1921), p. 232; also pp. 40, 164, 184. The *Vivekacudamani* construes experience as symptomatic rather than causal: 'The result of dispassion is Realisation,

...   that of Realisation is withdrawal from sense-pleasures, which leads to the experience of the Bliss of Self, whence follows Peace' (p. 184); experience is a 'proof' or 'test' of Realization (pp. 205–6). On Ramana's translation of the *Vivekacudamani*, see *The Mountain Path*, vol. 22, no. 4 (1985), pp. 252-8; Thomas A. Forsthoefel, 'Ramana Maharshi: Mystic as Translator', *Journal of Hindu Studies*, vol. 5, no. 2 (2001), pp. 127–8.

121   *'Why does man go out to look for a God?...'*: James, *Varieties of Religious Experience*, p. 504 (Lecture 20); he also cites a new collection of Ramakrishna's 'Life and Sayings' edited by the Sanskritist Max Müller, assisted by Vivekananda (pp. 354, 357). William James met Vivekananda – who 'constantly evoked' mystical experience – at 'philosophical soirées' in Boston in 1896, four or five years before he wrote *The Varieties of Religious Experience* – see Harris, *Guru to the World*, pp. 202–6.

122   *spiritual success required only the willingness to 'dive within' and question yourself*: See Forsthoefel, 'Ramana Maharshi: Mystic as Translator,' p. 112, and Thomas A. Forsthoefel, 'The Sage of Pure Experience: The Appeal of Ramana Maharshi in the West', *Journal of Hindu-Christian Studies*, vol. 14 (2001), pp. 31–36.

122   *drawn to perennial philosophies or inter-faith practice, or lured by an exotic 'alternative' to their own culture*: Thomas A. Forsthoefel, 'Weaving the Inward Thread to Awakening: The Perennial Appeal of Ramana Maharshi', *Horizons*, vol. 29, no. 2 (2002), pp. 240–59, 243. On 'exoticism' see Véronique Altglas, *From Yoga to Kabbalah: Religious Exoticism and the Logics of Bricolage* (Oxford: Oxford University Press, 2014), pp. 11–18.

122   *In a new century oppressed by the burden of choice ...*: 'The burden of choice' is a quotation from George Eliot's *Romola*, vol. 2 (London and Edinburgh: William Blackwood and Sons, 1878), p. 325 (chapter 61).

123   *'The divine ordainer controls the fate of souls in accordance with their past deeds ...'*: See B. V. Narasimha Swami, *Self Realisation: Life and Teachings of Sri Ramana Maharshi*, fifth edition. (Tiruvannamalai: Sri Ramana Ashram, 1953), p. 66.

123   *he responded that Gandhi had likewise surrendered to the divine*: See David Godman, 'Bhagavan and the Politics of his Day' (www.davidgodman. org/bhagavan-and-the-politics-of-his-day/)

123   *'He must do what he has come for. We must do what we have come for'*: See Mudaliar, *Day by Day with Bhagavan*, pp. 133–4 (2 February 1946);

... David Godman, *Nothing Ever Happened: A Biography of Papaji* (Boulder, CO: Avadhuta Foundation, 2017), vol. 2, pp. 298–9. Ramana taught that there was nothing wrong with political or social action, if it was done 'without the sense "I am the doer", but feeling: "I am the Lord's tool." Similarly one must not be conceited: "I am helping a man below me. He needs help. I am in a position to help. I am superior and he is inferior." But you must help the man as a means of worshipping God in that man.' – *Day by Day with Bhagavan*, p. 94 (5 January 1946).

124 *a universal notion of religion that 'transcends Hinduism' and seeks union with 'the truth within':* Quoted by Mohit Chakrabarti in *Gandhian Humanism* (New Delhi: Concept Publishing Company, 1992), pp. 54–5, from M. K. Gandhi, *Young India*, 12 May 1920. On Gandhi's discovery of Hindu traditions via British theosophists, see his *Autobiography* (London: Penguin, 2001), pp. 76–7; on his relation to Advaita Vedānta, see Douglas Allen, *Gandhi After 9/11: Creative Nonviolence and Sustainability* (Oxford: Oxford University Press, 2019), pp. 40–59.

124 *Both Gandhi and Ramana taught by example, a method that Gandhi regarded as essentially non-violent:* See Akeel Bilgrami, 'Gandhi, the Philosopher', *Economic and Political Weekly*, vol. 38, no. 39 (2003), pp. 4159–65. Bilgrami explains that Gandhi 'tried throughout his life to avoid criticism of individuals', while being prepared to criticize institutions, policies, and indeed modern western culture as a whole, and also while sometimes failing to live up to his own intention to avoid criticizing individuals. Annamalai Swami's account of life in the Ramana ashram contains numerous quotidian instances of Ramana refusing to take sides in disputes among his devotees, and instead teaching by his own example. If two devotees were blaming each other for leaving a room untidy, Ramana would begin to clean it himself – which inevitably prompted his devotees to rush to do the work for him.

124 *'had the most sattvic body I have ever seen ...':* Godman, *Nothing Ever Happened: A Biography of Papaji*, vol. 2, pp. 298–9. On Ramana's radiance, see also Isaac Portilla, 'Interfaith Dialogue and Mystical Consciousness', *Harvard Theology Review*, vol. 115, no. 4 (2022), pp. 591–620.

125 *I would love to know how it is that Brahman manifests as Arunachala – how an ocean creates a wave; how Spinoza's finite modes 'flow from eternity':* See Spinoza, Letter 12 in *The Collected Works of Spinoza*, vol. 1, p. 203. Spinoza tries to answer this question in *Ethics* I, P22–P28, where he suggests that the causal relationship between God and finite modes is mediated by two phases of infinite modes: first, the infinite intellect of

... God (under the attribute of thought) and motion and rest (under the attribute of extension); second, the face of the whole universe. Some Vedānta philosophers' answers to the same question are discussed by Jessica Frazier in 'What Kind of "God" Do Hindu Arguments for the Divine Show? Five Novel Divine Attributes of Brahman', *Sophia*, vol. 63 (2024), pp. 471–95.

127 *'no generation learns what is truly human from a previous generation ... every generation begins primitively'*: Kierkegaard, *Fear and Trembling*, pp. 108–9.

128 *'supra-worldly and intra-worldly at the same time'*: Zimmer, 'Die Schale der Persönlichkeit', p. 72.

130 *'My heart ached as I said goodbye ...'*: Celia Paul, *Self-Portrait* (London: Jonathan Cape, 2019), pp. 157–9.

131 *'All that had been structured and consoling before had broken up and dissolved ...'*: Paul, *Self-Portrait*, p. 184.

133 *'objectivity and detachment are the supreme aesthetic virtues'*: Maurois, *Aspects of Biography*, p. 63.

134 *when we ask, as a philosopher must, what is love?, the answer surely lies in this concept of devotion: at once an action, a feeling, a relationship and an affirmation of value*: Contemporary philosophers debating the nature of love tend to go for one of these conceptions; for an overview, see Bennett Helm, 'Love', *The Stanford Encyclopedia of Philosophy* Fall 2021 edition, ed. Edward N. Zalta. For an analysis of devotion, see Paul Katsafanas, *Philosophy of Devotion: The Longing for Invulnerable Ideals* (Oxford: Oxford University Press, 2023).

135 *'to need God is a human being's highest perfection'*: See S. Kierkegaard, *Eighteen Upbuilding Discourses*, trans. Edna H. Hong and Howard V. Hong (Princeton, NJ: Princeton University Press, 1992), pp. 297–326.

137 *The ancient Greeks called this devotional practice theoria*: See Nightingale, *Philosophy and Religion in Plato's Dialogues*, p. 21.

137 *Here he sets out a conversion narrative, in which he 'devotes' himself to 'the true good'*: See Spinoza's *Treatise on the Emendation of the Intellect* §1–14 in *The Collected Works of Spinoza*, vol. 1, pp. 7–11.

138 *human goodness that 'like a jewel, shines by itself'*: Immanuel Kant, *Groundwork of the Metaphysics of Morals*, trans. Mary Gregor

...   (Cambridge: Cambridge University Press, 1997), p. 8. Kant is talking about the good will; he argues that the concept of duty contains this concept of a good will 'under certain subjective limitations and hindrances [which] bring it out by contrast and make it shine forth all the more brightly' (p. 10).

139   *just as Proust's middle-aged narrator is transported to a series of past selves in past worlds, as their sensations recur...*: See Jean-Yves Tadié, *Marcel Proust: A Life* (London: Viking, 2000), p. 564.

139   *'Can I call this book a novel?'*; *'It is something less, perhaps, and yet much more, recounting the very essence of my life, with nothing extraneous added, as it could be felt flowing by'*: Tadié, *Marcel Proust: A Life*, pp. 282, 838; see Proust's *Jean Santeuil* (Paris: Pléiade, 1971), p. 181. On the novel's status as fiction, not (lightly fictionalized) autobiography, see Joshua Landy, *Philosophy as Fiction: Self, Deception, and Knowledge in Proust* (Oxford: Oxford University Press, 2004), pp. 14–24.

140   *'encompassing many deaths and many unrecognisable rebirths'*: See Eve Kosofsky Sedgwick, *The Weather in Proust*, ed. Jonathan Goldberg (Durham, NC: Duke University Press, 2011), p. 7.

140   *a 'wonderful day', on which 'the aim of my life and perhaps that of art were illuminated'*: Proust, *Time Regained*, pp. 235–6.

140   *'so many memories, so many joys and desires'; 'all this span of time ... was my life...'*: See Marcel Proust, *Time Regained*, pp. 433–4. On whether the novel the narrator intends to write is *In Search of Lost Time*, see Joshua Landy, *Philosophical Fictions*, pp. 36–47.

141   *'to bear it as a load, to accept it as the object of his life, to build it like a church ...'*: Proust, *Time Regained*, p. 415.

142   *Edward Casaubon, 'who had devoted his entire life to an insignificant and absurd study'*: See Proust, *Jean Santeuil*, p. 489, and Tadié, *Marcel Proust: A Life*: '[Proust] projected onto [Charles Swann] his own fear about not finishing his book, his Casaubon complex, his dread of being merely a *célibataire de l'art*' (pp. 269, 323).

142   *'a church where the faithful would gradually learn truth ...'*: Proust, *Time Regained*, p. 425.

144   *'he lived in order to write', and his own life – including his friendships – became a 'laboratory' to be used to that end, with all the ruthlessness this use*

... *implies*: See Tadié, *Marcel Proust: A Life*, p. 508; also p. 291: 'everything was put to use.'

145 *the loss of your self ... 'can occur very quietly in the world ...'*: Kierkegaard, *The Sickness Unto Death*, p. 33.

145 *'There is so much talk about wasting a life ...'*: Kierkegaard, *The Sickness Unto Death*, pp. 26-7.

146 *'simultaneously to be out on 70,000 fathoms of water and yet be joyful'*: S. Kierkegaard, *Stages on Life's Way*, trans. Edna H. Hong and Howard V. Hong (Princeton, NJ: Princeton University Press, 1988), p. 477.

146 *not some intrinsic or objective feature we discern in things*: On the concepts of intrinsic, objective and unconditioned goodness, see Rae Langton, 'Objective and Unconditioned Value', *The Philosophical Review*, vol. 16, no. 2 (2007), pp. 157–85.

Illustrations

Acknowledgements

This book took form first as six Gifford Lectures given at the University of St Andrews in March and April 2024. I would like to thank the St Andrews Department of Philosophy (and especially James Harris) for the invitation, and everyone who came to the lectures for their generous attention and great questions.

Thanks also to Joseph Sinclair, John Tresch, Celia Paul, Karen Kilby, David Godman, Miri Albahari, Jonardon Ganeri, Karen O'Brien-Kop, Judith Wolfe, Kieran Setiya, Charles Collier, John Cottingham, Jessica Frazier, Sarah Chalfant, Jessica Bullock, Amber Husain, Charlotte Jackson and Jacques Testard.

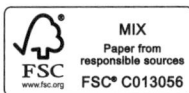

The authorized representative in the EEA
is eucomply OÜ, Pärnu mnt 139b-14,
11317 Tallinn, Estonia.
hello@eucompliancepartner.com
+337 576 90241

Fitzcarraldo Editions
133 Rye Lane
London, SE15 4ST
United Kingdom

ISBN 978-1-80427-195-7

Design by Ray O'Meara
Typeset in Fitzcarraldo
Printed and bound by Pureprint

fitzcarraldoeditions.com

Fitzcarraldo Editions